PRAYERS *And*
THOUGHTS

PRAYERS *And* THOUGHTS

A DEVOTIONAL FOR THE SICK AND THOSE WHO CARE FOR THEM

By Chaplain David Rapp, MAPS, BCC

Xulon Press

Xulon Press Elite
2301 Lucien Way #415
Maitland, FL 32751
407.339.4217
www.xulonpress.com

Scripture quotations taken from the New American Bible, Revised Edition (NABRE).
Copyright © 2011 by Confraternity of Christian Doctrine. Used by permission. All
rights reserved.

Printed in the United States of America.

Edited by Xulon Press.

ISBN-13: 9781545604892

DEDICATION

Dedicated to all my patients, all my companion caregivers and to my wife Sandi who has encouraged and healed my spirit with her prayers and love for fifty years.

TABLE OF CONTENTS

———————✺———————

"Prayer is a language of healing for both [patient and care-giver]." Indeed! And thank you, Chaplain David, for teaching us this language. What a great treasure to possess, in these pages, prayers that have been tried and tested on the sacred grounds of human suffering. These prayers sound the depths of the soul!

Deacon Frank DiGirolamo
Director of Deacons and Senior Priests - Archdiocese
of Seattle

In Prayers and Thoughts, Deacon David Rapp provides a wealth of prayer offerings for the care giver and receiver. They breathe life and love, and embody Deacon. Rapp's deeply held belief "that no matter the depth of mystery or confusion in a situation, God is always good and always near." Scripture, poetry, excerpts from our traditions, soothing reflections, and compassionate prayers fill this volume. Thank you, David, for giving us this invaluable rich resource.

David A. Lichter, D. Min.
Executive Director
National Association of Catholic Chaplains

Powerful! Full of compassion, empathy and faith! Deacon David Rapp shares in prayer what he has brought to his ministry for so many years as a chaplain and a Deacon. I whole-heartedly recommend Prayers and Thoughts for anyone who is ill and for their caregivers and families. Every chaplain and pastoral care volunteer should have this book in their kit.

Erica Cohen Moore,
Director of Pastoral Care and Leadership & Transition Ministry - Archdiocese of Seattle

Prayers and Thoughts, by Deacon David Rapp, provides words of comfort, compassion, healing and hope for all individuals who find themselves suffering with illness of body, mind and spirit. The depth of spirituality and years of working with those who are sick comes through David's prayers. Prayer #98 sums up the promise of God's healing: "This is the day you have made, Lord. Fill it with your grace...Fill it with your hope." Amen, David, to a timeless collection of prayers.

Dianna L Kielian, FACHE
Senior Vice President of Mission
CHI Franciscan

Each reflection and prayer speaks of hope and courage, of peace and of God's never-ending presence and love. These prayers and reflections can heal the spirit. This book is valuable for all health ministers and, in particular, for faith community nurses in their care and healing of people.

Debbi Saint, RN BSN
Coordinator, Congregational Health Ministries
CHI Franciscan

INTRODUCTION

There is a divine call to be healed, to be whole. A healed, whole self is our natural state. Anything less is an illness. Ever since Genesis we have been in a holy partnership with God in the care of all creation. Mother Teresa once said: "If we have no peace, it is because we have forgotten that we belong to each other". When we heal others, we are also healing ourselves; when we heal ourselves, we are also healing others; we are healing our community and bringing peace to it.

We need good caregivers, good family, good friends and, most of all, God's good grace, to relieve the stress and heal the fractures in body, mind or spirit that are caused by sickness and pain. The reflections and prayers in this book are written to restore peace and wholeness to body, mind and spirit. They will work to restore us to health in all the places of stress within us.

These prayers have been said in patient rooms. hallways, family rooms, meeting rooms, lobbies and operating rooms. Embedded in them is the belief that no matter the depth of mystery or confusion in a situation, God is always good and always near. These prayers have brought comfort and healing to many people. They have been printed in church bulletins and pinned to walls in patient rooms and meeting rooms. They have gone into surgery suites. In God's grace, share them with each other.

May they bring you comfort and healing.

SECTION I

Prayers for Patients

#1 - THIS I KNOW

REFLECTION:

> **I praise you, because I am wonderfully made;**
> **wonderful are your works! (Ps 139:14)**

Once, when my son was four months old and totally paralyzed and seemingly dying, my wife called me to prayer. "Let's pray!", she said. I was so overcome by what was happening that I could find no words of prayer. Finally, after a period of numb muteness I blurted out, "God, I know you exist!". This was perhaps one of the most profound prayers of my life. I had been reduced to a prayer of profound faith. I knew one thing only: God was Good and He was in Control!

PRAYER

Lord, this I know,
Even in the confusion of being sick,
    I know there is something
    You cannot do –

You cannot stop loving me!

I am Your creature
    Whom You have
    Wonderfully made and
    Wonderfully love.

No matter what I have done
    Or has been done to me,
You will be faithful
    In Your love for me today,

Tonight,
Tomorrow and
Forever –
    All the way into eternity.

I am reaching to You, Lord.
    In my sickness
    I need Your grace
    To help me.

Lord,
    Hold me;
    Comfort me;
    Heal me.

Help me to keep hope that mirrors
    Your love for me.

Lord, this I know:
    I am safe.
        I cannot fall out of Your love.

AMEN!

#2 - You Are My Shelter

REFLECTION:

> **You are my shelter; you guard me from distress;
> with joyful shouts of deliverance you surround
> me. (Ps 32:7)**

Sometimes a doctor will examine a foot or an arm and tell you that you have a stress fracture in your bones. Stress fractures can show up in any part of your life. Whenever something is too much for your spirit to bear, you can find yourself in the dark valley where trust is fractured and the vapors of fear threaten. As with any fracture in your body, you need good doctors, good family, good friends and, most of all, God's good grace, to relieve the stress and heal the fractures.

Take the troubles and worries that strain me, Lord. Restore peace and wholeness to my mind and body. Heal my spirit and heal my body in all the places of fracturing.

PRAYER

Heal the fractures that come from my worrying.
Grant that I may love more fervently.

Heal the fractures that comes from
The wounds of my broken relationships.
Grant me a forgiving ear and heart.

Heal the fractures that come from my anger.
Grant me a peaceful heart.

Heal the fractures that come from my guilt.
Grant me a repentant heart

I take refuge and give refuge in Your love.

Embrace me with Your healing mercy and love;
Let me reflect Your peace
To those who care for me and
To all who are around me.

Behind and before
Encircle me with healing peace.
Rest your hand upon me.

AMEN!

#3 - BEFORE MY BIRTH THE LORD CALLED ME

REFLECTION:

> ... From my mother's womb, he gave me my name. (Is 49:1)

By His own word, God cannot forget me, He says: Even should she (a mother) forget, I will never forget you! See upon the palms of my hands, I have engraved you. (Isaiah 49:16) No matter the state of my illness or injury, I can hold confident hope.

PRAYER

I am having trouble
    Finding the good in today.
I cannot see
    What there is to love about me.
That is why I must remember the story
    That began before my birth and
    That will not end with my death.

From my mother's womb
You gave me my name:
    I am Yours absolutely;
        I am precious absolutely.

AMEN.

#4 - COME TO ME, ALL YOU BURDENED ONES

REFLECTION

> **Take my yoke upon you and learn from me, for
> I am meek and humble of heart; and you will
> find rest for your selves. (Mt 11:29)**

Jesus says: "I have invited all of you who are burdened to
come to Me and I will give you rest. Why do you fear to risk
answering my invitation? Pride, resentment and fear seem like
protective responses but in reality only cause greater burden.
What I offer is counter-intuitive as is almost all of Christianity.
Disciplined humility and joy are the path to a resting spirit.
They take practice and prayer! Come and see for yourself."

PRAYER

Lord, here I am,
    With my burdens.
I have come to seek Your presence and
    Your companionship through this day.

I am sick.
    I long for Your healing presence today.

I am so tired,
    So weary ...
It is hard to find You.
Help me, Lord.

Fill my heart to overflowing with
    Healing gratitude for all the times
        I have known Your love

In the care given to me.

All my life You have blessed me, yet,
I confess, Lord, that
    I have at times been tempted to
    Resent even You and Your sweet yoke!

Help me to fend off resentments
    Caused by my own pride and fears.

My burden is lightened
    By the example of
    Your humility under suffering
        In the Garden of Gethsemane.

Stay and watch with me, Lord.
Grant me the sweetness of Your presence.

AMEN!

#5 - For Guidance – Lead Me, Lord

> **The LORD preceded them, in the daytime by means of a column of cloud to show them the way, and at night by means of a column of fire to give them light. (Ex 13:21).**

Sickness is a desert place. It feels like a place of captivity, a place where my power to act or even to make choices has been taken away! Feeling without hope in such a place, I sometimes stay there frozen in that place of captivity; I simply choose to surrender to circumstances, to surrender my power – paralyzed in the darkness where I cannot see - or I can follow the light that God holds out for me! I am reaching out to You, Lord: lead me.

Lord, God,
You are a God of power and Might.
I am reaching out to You
    Like a little child
        Trapped by the dark.

Be my pillar of fire to light my way,
    To mark my path,
        To be my safety.
I am trusting in You, Lord.

This day holds choices
    That are hard for me
        To understand and

Decisions that
Are overwhelming.

Grant me wisdom and hope.
Renew my simple faith and
Trust in your goodness, love and mercy.
Give me courage enough to take
    Those footsteps in the sand of the desert.
    Still my trembling spirit.
Heal me, Lord for my journey.
    Be present around me and in me.

Encompass me with Your blessing.
    Lead me out of this pain and illness that
        Hold me captive.
In your power, might and mercy,
Grace me
    With the peace,
    The freedom and
    The light of
        Your healing presence, Lord.
Lead me, Lord:
Guide me.

AMEN.

#6 - PRAYING IT FORWARD!

> Be hospitable to one another without com-
> plaining. (1Pt 4:9)

"Hospitable" is the word *"hospital"* with the letters *"b" and "e"* added into it. One is never obliged by gratitude but certainly one is called to it and prompted by it – even to the point of "paying it forward". Jesus says: "When I paid it forward from My Cross, I gave you the example."

The suffering of pain and illness can weary you and can make you feel ungrateful and cranky. Do not discourage those care-givers and visitors who have come for your healing and encour-agement. After all, as Paul wrote: "Do not neglect hospitality, for through it some have unknowingly entertained angels." (Hebrews 13:2)

PRAYER

O Generous God,
Grant me a hospitable heart today
    For my caregivers and visitors.

Let me know gratitude and be hospitality,
Trusting in the good intentions of those
    Who come to my bedside.

Grant me a spirit of patience and peace
    With those people and procedures
        I do not want to tolerate.

Let my hospitality
    Make their work
        And my healing
            Easier.

Let my thoughts, words and actions today
    Be reverent, compassionate and kind
    Toward all of my caregivers and visitors.

AMEN

#7 - Walking Through a Dark Valley

REFLECTION:

> **... Rejoice in hope, endure in affliction, persevere in prayer ... (Rom 12: 12)**

Jesus says: "My Child, I have promised that I will walk beside you in the dark valleys and the places of pain and fear, and that I shall give you courage with my rod and my staff. I want you to have more than courage — I want you to have joy and hope, too! Have the confidence to endure in your afflictions in My love.

Carry a heart full of hope knowing that I am at your side all the way through the valley and that you will taste the joy of victory when we have passed through.

Persevere in your prayer; I will persevere with my rod and my staff. I am with you always."

PRAYER

Lord, steady my spirit
  Through my sickness and fear.
Be my protector and guardian.

Your powerful protection is
  Reason for courage.
Your love for me is
  Cause for my hope
Strengthen me to endure this affliction
 Not in trembling and despair but
 In the peace of firm hope.

Remain at my side
 With your rod and your staff
  To strengthen my spirit.

Companion me through the day,
Watch with me through the night
 As I pray for Your will to be done,
  Knowing it is ever good.

AMEN.

#8 - FOR FAITH

REFLECTION:

**What will separate us from the love of Christ?
(Rom 8:35)**

Jesus says: "Know, my child, that I am with you.
Fear not your circumstances for nothing will drive me away
from you.
Distraction, discouragement and exhaustion attack your faith
and your ability to let yourself become My beloved.
When all earthly reasoning would deny My presence or even
My goodness, put on the eyes of faith that you may have a
heart of love. Believe that nothing can separate you from My
love. Let your heart seek faith!"

Prayer

As this day starts.
I raise the flag of faith within my heart
    To guide my every action
        And purpose.
Trust in You, Lord,
    Will be my standard.
I will keep faith, not fear,
Love, not self-interest.
Beloved not fractured,
    I will march through every minute
    With You at my side,
    With You as my guide.
The flag of faith will
    Keep me in Your love.
I pray today to remain in Your presence

In every action I take.
I pledge not to separate myself
From You today, Lord.
In the midst of things
That may frighten and grieve,
Guilt and shame.
I will take refuge
In Your power and might
Through any sorrows, pains,
Humiliations or fears
That I shall endure this day,
As You have pledged
To abide always with me, Lord,
I pledge to abide with You
Every moment of this day -
To believe in You,
Every moment of this day -
To trust in You,
Every moment of this day
O Lord!
Let no doubt or distraction
Separate me from Your love today!

AMEN.

#9 - LET ME BE HEALED BY YOUR WORD

> **Indeed, the word of God is living and effective**
> **... (Heb 4:12)**

Let us hear God's word today and be healed by it. That is one of the things I most often pray for – to hear the Lord - especially when I am in trouble, feel lost, am sick or in pain. I say, *"Lord, help me, show me, tell me what to do now."* And when I am sometimes unable to hear God's voice, I ask *"Where are you, God?"* as if He isn't here.
But He is.
His Word is among us.

Prayer

I know that
    God's Word heals –
        Yet I am not sure,
           Sometimes;

I need someone to remind me.
    O Lord, send Your Word
        Among us today.
Give me ears to hear
    And a heart ready for healing.

I pray that I may hear Your Word today;
Give me ears to hear it
    And a heart to recognize it.

I pray to hear Your Word
    In the hearts and voices of
    People who love me.
Give me ears to hear it
    And a heart to affirm it.

I pray also for my caregivers
    To hear God's Word
    In the hearts and voices of their patients.
Give them ears to hear it
    And hearts to witness it.

Lord God
My Healer and Protector,
My Shepherd,
I thank You for Your Word among us today.
Let me hear Your word today
    And be healed by it.

AMEN.

#10 - GOD-BE-WITH-ME

REFLECTION:

> **I believe that God is in me as the sun is in the color and the fragrance of a flower – the light in my darkness, the voice in my silence. - Helen Keller (1880-1968)**

Helen Keller was born unable to see or hear. She never saw the beauty of a flower. She never heard a human voice talking to her. She faced far greater challenges to faith and hope than the most of us do who have the affirming witnesses of sight and speech. She is an inspiration of profoundly courageous faith.

PRAYER

O God of Power, of Strength,
    Of Faithfulness
        God of my Hope,
O God who is present to me always,
    Present to me now,

Give me courage for the journey of this day.

Give me courage for the failures and
    Successes that will come today.

Give me hope to endure and to heal.

Give me endurance to hang in there with You
    As we walk this day – You and I.

Courage is easier
    When I have a strong grip
    On my faith
    And my hope
    And when I hold charity in my heart.

So, Lord, throughout this day, protect
    My faith in its mysteries,
    My hope in its distractions and
    My charity in its annoyances and troubles.

Yes, Lord, grant me courage and hope
    Like Helen Keller's
        – In the firm confidence that
        You are sufficient for today
        whatever it may bring.

AMEN.

#11 - UNDER THE UMBRELLA OF HIS LOVE

REFLECTION

> **You are my shelter; you guard me from distress; with joyful shouts of deliverance you surround me. (Ps 32:7)**

Fear is enemy to my wellness of soul and body. It stresses me in my body and in my soul.
Faith is one of the antidotes to the poison of fear.
Hope is another.
Knowing that I am beloved by God is the best antidote of all.
Today I place myself under the umbrella of God's love.

PRAYER

Lord, calm my spirit
    With Your Spirit of hope and peace.
Soothe my soul with Your love.
Cast out the fears that
    Bring sickness to my spirit and body.

Protect and heal me
    Under the umbrella of your love.

Restore me to wholeness
    So that safe
        In Your loving protection
I may serve You
        In humble gratitude and joy today.

AMEN.

#12 - NIGHT AND DAY YOU ARE MY STRENGTH

REFLECTION:

> **... whoever serves, let it be with the strength
> that God supplies... (1Pet 4:11)**

Both the dark cold of the night and the blazing brightness of the noonday sun can burden us beyond the strength of our will to persevere on our chosen path. St Paul refers to this when he says I don't really understand myself, for I want to **do** what is right, but I don't do it. .... (Romans 7:15) Relying solely on our own willpower, we are doomed to failure. Only by walking in the grace of God, can we persevere on the right path. The grace of God is our true strength.

PRAYER

Lord, what do You have in store for me today?
Whatever it is, Lord,
    Remain with me,
        Stay close,
            Be my strength.

You have watched with me
        Through the night;
Now walk with me
        Through the day.
Help me to deal with
    The tiredness, the discouragement,
        The pain and the illness
            That come my way.

When I feel
    Powerless,
        Lonely
            Or hurt,
        Refresh me with your grace!
When I ask why, Lord,
    Send me a comforting
        Sign of Your love.
When I ask how, Lord,
    Show me a confirming
        Sign of faith.
When I ask how long, O Lord,
    Grant me an encouraging
        Sign of hope.

When my spirit is burdened with worry,
        Still my heart.
Fill my heart with gratitude
    For Your goodness.
Night and day, You are my strength.
    I beg You;
    Supply my need.

AMEN!

#13 - Wait for Me, Lord,

Wait for the LORD, take courage; be stout-hearted, wait for the LORD,! (Ps 27:14)

Waiting places are without power – they are scary. They test my faithfulness in the infinite goodness of God. Only love can overcome the ravages of doubt and hopelessness on my spirit. I need You with me in my waiting places lest I succumb to the attacks on my faith and hope. Be with me, Lord in my places of waiting. Wait for me. Wait with me.

PRAYER

You have had great patience with me, Lord.
    But I have had a lot of trouble
        Being patient with You some days.
This is one of them.
Why do You move so slowly?
I believe that
    You have never forgotten me.
You say that
    You have permanently tattooed
        My name on the palm of Your hand.
You are the Father always
    Watching for the
        Return of Your prodigal child.
Your waiting for me never waivers.
Even when I have not believed in You,
        Or in myself,
            You have waited for me;
You have believed in me –

And kept waiting.
Wait for me, Lord, as I attempt to
     Gather my courage.
I don't really feel like I have
     A very stout heart today.
I am afraid of
     What might happen next.
I am really stuck here.
There don't seem to be
     Any good choices
     Left in my life right now.
What can I do with this mess?
What can You do with this mess?
How can we bring
     Anything good out of this?
Give me courage and a stout heart
     To believe through
     My doubt and pain.
My hope is in
     Your power and mercy.
I am waiting for You, Lord,
     As You are waiting for me.
Let us wait together.

AMEN.

#14 - Lead Me, Lord, Lead Me

Reflection

> **Teach me, LORD,, your way that I may walk in your truth. (Ps 86:11)**

There is nothing that shatters ambiguity like the truth. When we are lost or uncertain about which way to go a shot of truth is like an elixir of peace. The right decision becomes a certain and irresistible choice. For our life to be content and happy, we must be relentless in pursuing the truth.

Prayer

Lord, God of power and might,
Lead me through the mysteries of this day.
Help me find You present.

Open my eyes, Lord
    To see the miracles of the day and
    To be astonished by them.
It is right that I should praise You today
    And every single day
    That You gift me with.

Lord, You did not make me to stand alone.
    You made me to love You
        and my neighbor.
Let us help each other to healing,
    To holiness and

    To salvation.
    Grace us to encourage one another.

Bless us!
We are brother and sister,
    Spouse, parent and child.
    Lead us all to know
        Your healing presence here.
        Make known Your ways to us.

May every one of my actions today
    Each be a
        Sign of Your presence and
            Witness to Your guidance.

May every one of my actions today
    Be a living prayer of
    Gratitude and hope and
    Witness to the rightness of Your ways.

All glory, praise and honor be to You,
O Gracious and Merciful Lord,
Today and always.
    Guide me on the blessed path of Righteousness, faith and peace.

Lead me, Lord; lead me through this day.

AMEN!

#15 - Look Upon His Holy Mountain

His foundation is on holy mountains. (Ps 87:1)

I live near Mount Rainier. It is a 14, 000-foot-tall mountain – an unmistakable revelation of God's might, majesty and beauty. It is a guiding landmark for the soul as well as for maps. It is hard to think that something so huge can become invisible, but it does when the clouds are just right.

So does our God become sometimes invisible but always there to guide us if we can just see through the clouds. His might, majesty and beauty are always with us.

Prayer

Lord. You are the Mighty One, the Creator,
    The One Who Orders All Creation,
        The One Who Holds it all together.

Your strength and beauty are
    Like the mighty and beautiful mountain
    You have planted so near.

Like You, our mountain is always there but
    Sometimes it is invisible
    Veiled in clouds;
Yet I know it is always there.

I depend on it to navigate my days
Just as I depend on You to navigate my life.

Do not hide Your face from me today, Lord.
Let Your mountain tower over
　　The clouds that may obscure my path
　　　　– clouds of pain, of sickness
　　　　– clouds of resentment
　　　　– clouds of unforgiveness,
　　　　– clouds of discouragement
　　　　– whatever clouds there may be
　　　　　　In my path today.

Standing firm in my faith and hope,
I turn to You in prayer this morning.
I call out to You.
I count on You.
Lead me through this day
Open the clouds.

Shine the light of Your face upon me and
Bless me from Your holy mountain
With faith, with hope and with charity
　　Sufficient for this day.

AMEN.

#16 - You Are Ever Near, Lord

Reflection

I am with you always. (Mt 28:20)

Just before Jesus ascended into heaven, He commissioned His apostles to go to all nations, to the ends of the Earth. He promised to be with them wherever they went and for all time. It is essential medicine for our souls to remember His promise when we feel lost or abandoned from His presence

Prayer

My spirit is disturbed
    When I cannot see Your footprints
        Beside mine, Lord.
When I cannot feel Your embrace, Lord,
    My spirit shudders in a great sigh

I am quieted within
    When I ponder on
    All of Your great deeds of the past.

I am refreshed to remember
    Hugs and embraces of strangers
        And of dear ones
        Whom You have sent
        To announce Your presence.

I tremble and fear now until
    I remember these things and know
        You have stood beside me
        And before me

So many times
With Your rod and Your staff;
And they give me courage and strength
For this day.
I will walk this day
By Your grace, and
In Your grace
Praising You for Your
Constant kindness and goodness to me.

There are days mysterious to me
Beyond my vision
In their pain and happenings, Lord;
They make me hesitant of Hope –
Unsure of myself, Lord,
And of You.
They bring me to doubt
Almost everything that
I think I know or understand, Lord;
But this I do know and will never doubt –
And it is enough for today:
I know You love me:
I know I love You:
I know You are always with me!

AMEN.

#17 - You Are My God

**You shall be my people; I shall be your God.
(Jer 30:22)**

No less than seven times does this promise appear in the scriptures. Through Abram, and later through Jesus, it is a promise of kinship – kinship with God!

It is because we are family that we can lay claim to God's protection and blessing and He can claim our faithfulness. Astounding!

PRAYER

I am Your treasure
    Whom You ever watch over.
From the first beat of my heart
    In my mother's womb,
You have
    Tended to me and
        Cared for me.
You rejoiced
    When I took my first breath of air.
You can number
    My every heartbeat,
    My every breath.
Faithfully, ever faithfully
    You have counted them with me.

You are closer to me than

My own heartbeat,
My own breath.
Every breath I draw is
Your gift to me.

And yet I do not know You –
Incapable of comprehending
Your greatness, Your power,
Your love, Your mercy,
Your forgiveness,
Your beauty ...
And yet You are
Within me and
Around me –
Ever faithfully present.

I am Your treasure:

Through joy and sorrow,
Grief and happiness,
In the dark valleys and
At the banquet tables,
You are ever near me.

Nothing can separate me from You.

AMEN.

#18 - The Infinity of Love

Reflection

Before the mountains were born,
the earth and the world brought forth,
from eternity to eternity you are
God. (Ps 90:2)

There is no measure sufficient for God – neither large nor small – yet our tiny hearts can contain Him. There are no means by which His presence can be portioned out – yet our small hearts can know him.

Mystery within mystery – Love within Love. Known but not defined. You are God without beginning or end.

Prayer

O Lord, You have been my
    Faithful refuge of love and mercy
    Present to me from all generations

Lord, You are faithful to me beyond time.
    A thousand years, a single day –
        It is all one.
            You are One.

Your faithfulness is forever now;
Immeasurable by *"was"* or *"will be"*.

You are the mystery of
 Love without measure,
 Strength without limit,
 Compassion without exhaustion,
 Hope without reason end,
  Life without end.

Each sunrise is a renewal of Your promise,
 A refreshment for my hope.
In the end ...
  All will be well.

Send me some joy today
  To balance the afflictions
  I am suffering.
Send me some hope today
  To balance the grief and loneliness
  I am enduring.

Walk with me today, Lord,
  Holding my hand,
  Steady at my side.
I long for Your presence.

AMEN!

#19 - I Am Your Child, Father, I Trust You

REFLECTION

For the LORD, comforts his people and shows mercy to his afflicted. (Is 49:13)

Here I am, Lord, simply trusting You.

Presence is intentional as is absence.
Today I choose to make myself present to God as He makes Himself present to me. I cannot see You, but I know You with the ears of my soul and the eyes of my heart. I choose to live present to You as You choose to walk this day present to me. How special is Your faithfulness that even death will not "separate us.

PRAYER

Father God,
Our Father,
My Father ...

I am Your child...

Give me a child's ears for today,
     That I may hear You when You call.
Give me a child's eyes,
     That I may see You when you come.
Give me a child's heart, that I may

     Love You with joy when things go wrong. ...
          When I hurt,
          When I am lonely,

When I am afraid,
When I am depressed,
When I am helpless,

Look on me
     With Your loving eyes,
     With Your loving heart.
Do not let any burden I experience today
     Blind me to Your presence
     Or deafen me to Your voice.

Comfort and sooth my spirit
     When I am troubled.
Replace my fears and troubles
     With Your peace.
Reach down and help me, Father.
Reach down,
Gather me up and
Hold me in safety.

I am Your child, Father.
Take my hand and walk this day with me.
I am Your child.
I trust You, Father.

AMEN!

#20 - Seek God's Face

"Come", says my heart, "seek his face". (Ps 27:8)

It was cloudy this morning with thick, low, tree-top-brushing clouds. The season is changing.

This reminded me that we are in a period of turmoil now in Health Care and also reminded me of the great changes that every one of my r patients is enduring in their own life as they deal with their illness.

Changes in my life and in my circumstances are often accompanied by clouds that obscure the landmarks from which I take my bearings.
So it is with the face of God. I cry out, *"Where are You, Lord.?"*
And I seek His steadying presence that is the landmark for my soul.

Prayer

Lord, it has become difficult, to see
    What is happening
    Beyond the illness and the pain
    That are in-my-face right now.
The mystery of it all,
    The not-knowing and the worry
    Are getting me on edge

And anxious.
I am beginning to feel isolated from everyone –
    The people taking care of me,
    The people I love
    And even a little from You, Lord.

Come, now, Lord!
Come out of the clouds.
I await You!
I am clinging to Your words in Psalm 46:
    "Be still ...
    Be still and know that
    I am God." (Psalm 46:10)
Like Your rod and Your staff,
    These words give me strength and courage:

I have lost my bearings
    Because of the clouds of my sickness:
    Let me see Your face, Lord!

Do not hide your face from me;
    Do not forsake me, God my savior!
LORD, show me Your way; ...
  "Wait for the Lord, take courage; be stouthearted, wait for
    the Lord!" (Ps 27:14)
I am waiting for You, Lord.

Lord, help me this morning to
    To Be Still and know that
    You are my God.

AMEN.

#21 - Your Goodness Does Not Change

> Cold and chill, bless the Lord... Frost and chill, bless the Lord. Hoarfrost and snow, bless the Lord! Praise and exalt Him forever! (Dan 3:67, 69-70)

These verses remind me that God's goodness is imprinted in all of Creation, even in the cold and ice. I don't like the cold. I don't like the ice – though others can find great joy in snow and ice, I am motivated to pray for a change.

Change happens all the time in our lives.
Every day we experience change: changes in weather, changes in our health, changes in our relationships, changes at work and at home. We welcome some changes; as we seem to catch a glimpse of You at work. We are grateful for answered prayer. And then there are changes that seem so overwhelming that all we can do is pray to the God of the Impossible.

Prayer

I don't understand
    And am
        Confused what You are doing, Lord.

Some changes
        I fear and they leave me wondering
        How You will keep me safe, Lord.

In the midst of the ever-constant
        Changes in my life and

In my world,
> I rely on Your unchanging love.

Today, increase my faith and hope
> In Your presence and
> In Your unchanging love for me.

Preserve me from all evil:
Protect me from being overloaded by
> Too much confusion,
> Too much doubt or
> Too much anxiety.

Do not allow more than I can handle today:
Be my strength and protection now and always.

Confident in Your faithful and unchanging love,
> I give You praise.
> With sure faith and hope,

I know you are the God of the Impossible.

"From the rising of the sun to its setting,
> Let the name of the LORD be praised!" (Ps. 113:3)

AMEN.

#22 - I Will Be with You Always

When you pass through the waters. I will be with you; through rivers, you shall not be swept away. ... For I, the LORD, am your God, the Holy One of Israel, your savior. (Is 43:2-3)

It is difficult to give my heart totally to God. It seems there are always worries, anxieties and resentment trying to creep in to the empty or irritated places in my heart.

Why is the temptation so great to abandon myself to things that are not from God? Lord, I wish to abandon myself to the safety of Your love.

PRAYER

I praise You for Your glory
    And Your power, Lord God.
I rely on Your compassion and mercy.
I trust in Your faithfulness to Your promises.
I desire to live in Your love.

But, still there is
    A space in my heart
    Taken by anxiety and worry.
They creep in
    Even as I stand in Your presence, Lord -
    Spaces where I am anxious about
        Myself,
        My family and
        My dear friends.

It seems there is much in this world
    That makes me anxious:
My health and
    My safety -
        My own or someone I love

I fret and grieve about
    Injured relationships,
        And wrong relationships, -
        About forgiveness –
    About grief and loneliness,
    About the rent and the car payment...
    My children ...
    There are many things, Lord.

Lord God, I bring all of my worries to You.
    Hear my pleas, O lord!
I praise You –
    Kind, merciful and compassionate
Beyond my ability to imagine.
You are all powerful, God.

I count on you, Lord,
    To take care of me
For I am Your child.

AMEN!

#23 - The Cloak of Your Love Around Me

> Oh, the depth of the riches and wisdom and
> knowledge of God! How inscrutable are his
> judgments and how unsearchable his ways!
> For who has known the mind of the Lord or
> who has been his counselor? (Rom 11:33-34)

Faith tells me that when life is
beyond my understanding,
God is near and keeps faith with me.
Hope tells me not to despair when events seem to have taken
away my power to speak or, seemingly, even to breathe.
It is **LOVE** that keeps my soul alive.

PRAYER

Heavenly Father,
Place the cloak of Your love over me today.
Though I may find myself faltering
    From fear or regret or even
    The heavy burdens of
      loneliness,
        anger or doubt,

I know You shall not take away Your love for me.

Heavenly Father,
Place the cloak of Your love over me today.

AMEN.

#24 - MARANATHA HEALING

Maranatha. The grace of the Lord Jesus be with you. (1Cor16:22-23).

Our bodies are infected by illnesses in our soul, by the trembling, fearful, grieving and sorrowing of our heart. And our soul is affected by pain and illness in our body. A broken bone, a cancer, a failing liver can bring fear, regrets or grief to our heart. Illness and accident assault our whole selves. Expectant hope is a catalyst for healing. "Maranatha" is expectant hope: it is two Aramaic words that mean "Our Lord comes". Maranatha, let us ask Your healing for our whole selves. Our Lord comes!

PRAYER

O God, awaken me to Your presence
    Here this morning.

Use me today, Lord, as both
    Your partner and Your servant.
Lord, make me a witnesses to life,
    A witness to Your caring.

You have made me wonderfully
    Both body and spirit, Lord.
I pray for healing of
    Whatever afflicts my soul and body today.
        Make me whole, Lord.
        Maranatha!

I know that my life began and
Continues in Your love and generosity.
And so I am praying to You, Lord,
The One Who was,
Who is and
Who always will be
The source of my life.

Maranatha!

You were with me yesterday.
You are here with me now.
You will be with me tomorrow.
I praise and thank You.

Maranatha!

Come, Lord,
Heal me today.

Maranatha!

AMEN.

#25 - BECAUSE OF THE LORD'S GREAT LOVE

REFLECTION

> **But this I will call to mind; therefore I will hope:**
> **The LORD's acts of mercy are not exhausted,**
> **his compassion is not spent;They are renewed**
> **each morning—great is your faithfulness!**
> **(Lam 3:21-23)**

Have you ever smelled the dawn or seen the perfumed beauty of a fresh-mown field of hay? Such is the experience of falling into God's love. It is breath-taking. It is new every morning!

PRAYER

Lord, though the day is new,
   Your faithfulness is not.

From the womb You have been
   Faithful to me.
      Constant.
         Never-changing.

You are fresh with me this morning.
I celebrate Your great love!

These things I know:
      You are ever faithful,
      Ever loving,

      Ever compassionate,
      Always good and
      Never changing.

Every night of my life You have watched at my bedside
    Waiting for me to awaken,
    Waiting to walk beside me on
    The path of our new day.

I thank You and praise You for Your faithful love.
I am counting on Your love and compassion to
    Hold me safe today.

You are my sunrise and my sunset,
    My sure hope for this day and
    All the days of my life
    Because of Your great love!

AMEN.

#26 - LORD, YOU ARE BEAUTIFUL!

> **Serve the Lord with gladness; come before him with joyful songs. (Ps 100:2)**

No one feels beautiful when they are sick.
Being sick has that effect on our spirit.
What does it mean to be beautiful? To be perfect?

It really gets in our face to realize that we are less than perfect.

The fact is we **ARE** made perfect – in God's own image! We are beautiful and beloved! When we celebrate God's beauty, we celebrate our own beauty. Do not sicken your spirit with thoughts of "ugly". Think rather on the beautiful creature that you are. Joyfully and gratefully give praise, honor and glory to your God.

PRAYER

Beautiful God, we are Your people,
    The flock You shepherd.
You have made us
    In Your image and likeness –
    All nations of this Earth:
    The peoples from the North, the South, the
        East and the West;
    The people of power and
    The people of affliction;
    The strong and the weak;
    The healthy and the ill;
    The newborn and the dying;

The Youth and the Elders.
We are Your people, Lord –
    Beautiful in Your sight.
We are Your people
    Made beautiful in Your likeness;
    Made brother and sister –
    Made of Your breath.
We are Your people
    The people of all nations;
    The people of all places;
    The people of all times;
    Sharing the breath of life
        Which You have breathed into us
Beautiful in Your sight.
We are your people
Who praise You this morning
With our every thought and breath of this day
    We will give You honor.
For You are Beautiful, Lord.
Your beauty endures forever,
Continues through all nations and generations
Continues in me
    For You are beautiful!

AMEN.

#27 - Grace-full Hearts - Peace-full Spirits

Reflection

You anoint my head with oil; my cup overflows.
(Ps 23:5b)

Blessed is the person who prays for holiness, for they shall receive in overflowing measure. The mystery of each day opens like a shelled nut. Shall we find sweet moist nut meat or a bitter and dry worm?

Sometimes it seems that we prophesy our days by our attitude. Gratitude, courage and hope are predictors of good outcomes.

Prayer

Lord of the Night,
God of the Dawn,
Ruler of the Day,

I approach You with gratitude that
    You have watched over me
        Through the night and
        With thanksgiving
        For the light You send at dawn
        To guide my steps today.

I will live into the mysteries of this day
With confidence
In Your love and goodness.
Protect my hope and faith and
Guard the charity in my heart
From being wounded by too much

Anxiety or pain.

Give me the courage that I need
To stand by You in reverence.
Give wisdom to my spirit
To find and hold hope
Sufficient for all trials.

Take all the worries and pains
That are in my heart and
Salve them with the ointment of
        Your generous mercy.

Lead me forth into this day with a
Grace-full heart and a
Peace-full spirit.

All honor and glory be Yours today and forever!

AMEN.

#28 - FAMILY

He went down with them and came to Nazareth, and was obedient to them... And Jesus advanced in wisdom and age and favor before God and man. (Lk 2:51)

Family is where we first learn that we are loved - where we first learn how to love and to be loved. Family is where we first learn how to be cared for and how to care for others. Jesus himself was born into a holy family where He was loved, cared for and protected by Mary and Joseph. Family bonds are the greatest blessings of human life. Let us give thanks to God for our families today and pray His protection and blessing upon them.

PRAYER

Lord, I pray today for all husbands and wives,
    All mothers, fathers, children,
    Brothers, sisters and grandparents.
That you will protect their families,
    Heal all their estrangements and
    Nurture their bonds of love and
    Faithfulness to each other.

Being sick makes me think of my own family
    And the graces that we need

Where forgiveness is needed,
Grace us
    To give it and

To accept it
    For the healing of our family.

Yes, Lord,
Make me Your instrument of
    Healing in my family.

Grant me wisdom;
Grant me humility,
Grant me courage,
And grant me love.

I pray this prayer in gratitude for the
    Many Blessings
    You have given to me
    And the many more You will pour upon me.,

AMEN.

#29 - Good Morning, God

> **All the days of the earth, seedtime and harvest, cold and heat, Summer and winter, and day and night shall not cease. (Gen 8:22)**

There is a solidarity that develops between patient and caregiver that often finds its way into their prayers. The one heals the other in affection and companionship as day follows day. Every day is a blessing.
Patient and Caregiver, let us pray for one another today.

PRAYER

Good morning, God.
Lord, be our encouragement today.
It is the beginning of a new day,
    Of a new week.
Be our hope for the unknown
    That is contained in today.

Most of all, Lord, we ask You to just be here.
    Be here with us.

And send us people who will be with us and
    Listen to us and
    Speak to us
    In ways that will reveal Your presence.

May the words that we speak be
Encouragement and hope to others and
May theirs be encouragement and hope to us.

May we build up faith in each other and
May we be channels of Your grace
    For each other.

As we touch each other's souls,
    May we make each other whole, healed.

Use each of us, caregiver and patient,
    To be like Your angels —
    Messengers of healing today!

We thank You and we bless You, Lord.

AMEN

#30 - THE WORD OF CHRIST AMONG US

> **Thus faith comes from what is heard, and what is heard comes through the Word of Christ. (Rom 10:17)**

That is one of the things we most often pray for. Isn't it – to hear the Lord among us - especially when we are in trouble, feel lost, are sick or in pain. We say, "Lord, help me, show me, tell me what to do now."
And when we are sometimes unable to hear God's voice, we ask "Where are you, God?" as if He isn't here.

In humility, our prayer must be that we allow ourselves to be God's Word for others. We can be God's Word for others because we are creature, made in the likeness of the Creator. It is no surprise that He uses us to sometimes speak His Word to others – brother, sister, spouse, neighbor or even stranger. He does; Yet we are not sure. Sometimes; we need someone else to remind us. *"Lord, send your Word among us today."* *(cf. Jn 1:14)*

PRAYER

Let me hear Your Word this morning, Lord.

Let me hear Your voice
As loudly as my own heart
Pulsing within me.

Let me hear Your Word in
The hearts and voices
Of those who love me
In the hearts and voices
Of those who care for me.

Whether I am
Caregiver or patient,
Speaker or listener,
Let me look for the words
You place among us today.
Let me
Speak them,
Listen to them and
Be encouraged and
Healed by them today.
You are near.
Let me hear You.

Lord, God, my Healer and Protector, my Guide,
I thank You for
Your Word among us today.
Help me to hear Your Word today
And be healed by it.

AMEN.

#31 - I Depend on Your Presence

Reflection

"Do not let your hearts be troubled. You have faith in God; have faith also in me." (Jn 14:1)

In the fourteenth chapter of the Gospel of John, the disciples struggle with their faith in Jesus. Thomas asks: "Master, we do not know where you are going; how can we know the way?" And Philip said to Him, "Master, show us the Father, and that will be enough for us."
We are not so different from the disciples. There are times we worry and times we question.
Jesus reassures his disciples with: "I am the way and the truth and the life. No one comes to the Father except through me. If you know me, then you will also know my Father."
Jesus is the Way, the Truth and the Life; this is our faith; this is our hope.

PRAYER

You are an eternal God, Lord,
A God Who is beyond time.
A God who I do not,
     Cannot,
     Yet understand.

I live in today
     A place that has a sunrise and a sunset
     A place where I believe You are but
     A place where I often cannot see You
     A place where I hope to find You but
     Sometimes wonder.

Be with me, Lord.
Let me see You today!

My illnesses and trials make it hard
     To know and see Your presence;
But I depend on Your presence
     For meaning and comfort.

I need You!

Come walk beside me, Lord.
     Make strong my faith
     In Your presence and love;

Soothe my spirit and body
     In the bath of Your peace.
Make Your healing known!
Make Your consolation felt!
     Today, and now!

AMEN.

#32 – Increase of Faith, Hope and Charity

Reflection

> He said to her, "Daughter, your faith has saved you. Go in peace and be cured of your affliction." (Mk 5:34)

Whether I am patient or caregiver, healing takes a lot of strength and courage, a lot of faith and a lot of hope; and these are not sustainable without love, without charity in my heart. So I pray today that the Lord will strengthen me for healing.

PRAYER

Lord, grant me faith,
    Hope
        And love
    Sufficient for today
        And the trials it brings.

Lord, give me the ability to find Your presence
    In the face of today's mysteries.

Lord, give me the ability to laugh and
    To shed tears with You
        In the grace of Your love
        That binds us together and
        Enables me
        To heal and to be healed.

The Lord is my Shepherd.

In the mystery that is today,
    Through the dark valleys
    Where I may not be able
    To see His presence,
    He shall lead me to healing.

I will live in His presence today and
    All of my days
        For years to come.

AMEN.

#33 - On My Bed I Remember You

REFLECTION

**O God, You are my God; it is you I seek.
(Ps 63: 1)**

One of the most profound statements one can make is claiming God to be "**my** God." Through the ages these two simple words have touched many people: "My God!"
They are so appropriate today here in this hospital (sick room) where I struggle with these circumstances in which I now find myself.
When I am in "desert" times, I actually feel like I am in a "dry and thirsty land": I seek out memories of better times and places.

Like me, the psalmist ponders how when he feels far away from secure places and memories. When I am flat on my back in a sick bed in the middle of the night, I can still know that God is with me and for me and that God gives me the strength to say: "O God, You are my God".

PRAYER

On my bed I remember You;
    I think of You through the
        Watches of the night.
Because You are my help,
I sing in the shadow of Your wings.

My soul clings to You;
    Your right hand upholds me.

Lord, help me remember that
    Even in the desert times
    I am sheltered by the shadow of Your wings.
    For You are my God!

Let me sense the strength of
    Your strong right hand
    Holding me up.
    For You are my God!

Lord, grant me today the knowledge that
    You are for me.
    For You are my God!

Lord, remind me today that
    You shelter me in these desert places.
    For You are my God!

Lord, let me feel Your strength
    Holding me up when I am weak.
    For You are my God!

AMEN.

#34 - LOVE NO-MATTER-WHAT

REFLECTION

We love because he first loved us. (1Jn 4:19)

This is a "quid pro quo" world; "Scratch my back; and I'll scratch yours." That's the way that so much of the world works. Always it seems we have to earn what we want.
But that's not the way the kingdom of God works. "We love because He first loved us." While we were still sinners He loved us. He loved us no matter what.
Whether we love Him or hate Him, Jesus loves us. His is a no-matter-what love. We do not earn it. It is free – totally gratuitous.

PRAYER

Lord, God, I remember
    Your love for me.
    In times of trouble and worry,

I remember that You loved me first and more.
I remember that You love no-matter-what.

I remember
    That it was You
        Who tenderly knitted me together
        In my mother's womb;
        Who danced with delight
            On the day I was born.

I remember that it is
    You who has walked
    Every single day of my life with me,
    Watched over me every night of my life
    While I slept.

You have loved me from the beginning.
    Constantly.
        Faithfully.
            Without change.
Help me to love as You love. -
    Help me to love without fear.

Grace me to live today in love with You.

Because of my love for You and
    Yours for me
        I will live today
        In peace with myself
        And with others.

I can love no-matter-what
    Because You have loved me
    First and more!

AMEN.

#35 - This Stormy Day

Reflection

Cast all your worries upon him for he cares for you, (1Pet 5:7)

On windy days, sailors are very aware of the importance of having a good anchor to rely on. Anchors are ancient in their use and ancient in their symbolism. They are symbols of hope, of something to steady your boat during a storm.
That is what hope does for us.

Hope is what we need when we are caught in the storm of illness. Healer, patient, family — we all need hope when we do battle with illness and injury.

Healer and patient, family and friend, let us anchor ourselves in hope today.

PRAYER

My hope is in the Name of the Lord
   Who has made heaven and earth.
My hope is in the Lord
   Who has made me and
   Preserves me in love.

My hope is in the Lord who only wills my good.
I take hope in His Goodness and Mercy today.

As there is always mystery in a storm,
So there is mystery in the ways of God
   That seem beyond my understanding.

But this I do know:
In all mystery,
     I can trust His Goodness.

Lord God, come and steady me today.

Lord God, send Your angels to be with me today,
   Send them to protect, to guard, to guide me
   In the stormy winds of mystery.

I ask Your blessings of hope and healing today,
   This stormy day.

AMEN.

#36 - The Kind Rule of God

The LORD will guard you from all evil; he will guard your soul.

The LORD will guard your coming and going both now and forever. (Ps 121: 7-8)

"From where shall come my help?" This is a question we often ask when we are ill and in pain. It is also the question answered in Psalm 121:2. "My help comes from the LORD,the maker of heaven and earth." Our God is full of kindness and mercy.

PRAYER

From where shall come my help?
From You, Lord!
    You have made me
    And privileged me
    To know Your kind rule.

Grant me a heart that is at peace with all whom
    I speak to, listen to, work beside and
    Care for and
        With those who care for me.

Grant me a heart and soul that are at
    Peace with You today,
A heart that is willing to ask for and accept

    Your mercy and love
        And your kind rule.

Grant me a heart and soul that are at peace
    So that there is room for
        Your compassion and presence

Grant me a heart and soul that
    Anchor me in Your presence
    No matter what trouble I may face today.

Grant me a heart and soul that are
    Beacons of peace in this place of healing

Blessed by Your help and protection, Lord,
    I face this day, this little piece of eternity,
    With a peaceful and thankful heart.

My help is from You, the Lord
    Who made heaven and earth!

AMEN.

#37 - A Prayer for All Patients and Staff

Reflection

Encourage yourselves today, while it is still "today" ... (Heb 3:13)

In our prayer today, let us especially give thanks to God for each other. Let us bless each other. We are gift and blessings to each other. Be thankful to God for the gifts and talents we have individually and thankful for the gifts and talents for healing that we have as a team of caregivers and patients. The fruit of our working together is healing. Healing is cause for our rejoicing and encouragement in our work.

PRAYER

The LORD bless you and keep you!
The LORD let his face shine upon you,
and be gracious to you!
The LORD look upon you kindly
and give you peace! (Num 6:24-26)

AMEN!

#38 – HE BEARS MY BURDENS

> Bless the LORD, my soul; and do not forget all
> his gifts, who pardons all your sins, and heals
> all your ills. (Ps 103: 2-3)

Whether I am a patient or a caregiver, a sick room can be a place where we reflect on the burdens of life.

This can be discouraging; but with skilled and compassionate caregivers, with faith and hope in God, the sickroom is a place where we can look for restoration and for healing of our whole selves – of our body, of our mind and of our spirit.

Hope heals.

PRAYER

Pray with me these words of Psalm 68:
Blessed be the Lord day by day,
God, our salvation,
Who carries us.j
Our God is a God who saves. (Ps 68:20-21a)

Yes, my God is with me.
My God is faithful
Even when I am not.

When I feel unloved, unlovable,
He is still loving me into existence.

Blessed be the LORD day by day,
God, our salvation, who carries us. (Psalm 68:20)

Lift my burdens, Lord.
Let me know Your presence today, Lord.
Let me know Your mercy today, Lord.
Let me know Your healing today, Lord.

Restore my hope.
My gratitude is confident;
Evening shall find me praising You!

As You bless me
I Bless You!

AMEN.

#39 - Wisdom and Grace

Reflection

> Do not be wise in your own eyes, fear the LORD
> and turn away from evil;
> This will mean health for your flesh and vigor
> for your bones. (Prov 3: 7-8)

Both patient and caregiver draw from a cauldron of grace and wisdom. Cling to your wisdom.

Sickness, whether it be your own or someone else's, can infect your spirit and rob you of your wisdom. Good health requires wisdom and reverence for self and for God. Reverence and gratitude loose the graces of mercy

PRAYER

Wisdom of God,
Be with me today,
That I may be a good healer,
That I may be healed

Mercy of God,
Be with me today,
That I may heal,
That I may be healed

Healing power of God,
Be with me today,
Working within me,
Working through me.

Shepherd God,
Merciful God,
Protect and heal me this day.

I ask your blessed presence and help this day.

AMEN.

#40 - The Lord Upholds My Life

Reflection

> **O God, by your name save me, and by your might defend my cause. O God, hear my prayer; hearken to the words of my mouth. (Ps 54: 3-4)**

Whether I am patient or caregiver, I need a champion, Lord. You are my protector.
Whether I am patient or caregiver, I need a guide, Lord. You are my shepherd.

Your rod and Your staff strengthen and lead me.

Prayer

Truly, Lord, You are my hope and my strength.

Please hear my prayer, Lord.

Sustain my life and
    The lives of those whom I so dearly love.
        Bring healing to our bodies,
        Bring peace to our minds,
        Bring vigor to our spirits.

Guard the souls of all in this sickroom -
    Patients and caregivers,
    Families and friends.

Help us to always be
    Compassionate and excellent.
Help us to use well the
    medicines and machines that we have
        For healing.

Teach us also how to use
    The most powerful instruments of healing
        That you have given us:
            Eyes that welcome,
                Ears that accept,
                    Hearts that care and
                        Hands of soft and
                        Powerful grace.

Truly, Lord, You are my hope and my strength.
Truly, Lord, You uphold my life!

AMEN.

#41 - Some Time, Lord, Please

Reflection

**But do not ignore this one fact, beloved, that
with the Lord one day is like a thousand years
and a thousand years like one day. (2Pet 3:8)**

Spend time, lose time, make time, find time, save time. Time is
a gift. We do not control it; we use it. Use it or not, it happens.
Take it or not; it is a gift.

Time is important to us. It is how we measure our lives, our
history. Fortunately, our God is beyond time. When we - when
things - are out of control, He is in control. With His grace, time
is bridged to eternity. Our hope is in the name of the Lord, the
God of All Time.

Prayer

Lord, God, You are Creator of our world,
    Of our lives,
        Yet beyond our space,
        Beyond the time by which
            I measure myself and my life.

Everything I know, Lord,
    Has measure
    - Except You.
Everything I know, Lord.
    Has beginning and end
        Except You.

You are more than sufficient.
You are more than infinite.
You are great and glorious
    Beyond my comprehension.

My hope rests in Your greatness.

Lead me
    Through the minutes and hours of this day.
        Be at my side as I wait my way
            Through them.

You are truly my rod and my staff
    You give me courage.

Your ways, Your goodness,
    Your kindness and Your mercy
        Are beyond my understanding

You are my hope!
    Be with me through each minute and
    Each hour of today.

AMEN.

#42 - DAYLIGHT IS HERE NOW

> **My soul waits for the Lord more than sentinels for daybreak. More than sentinels for daybreak, let Israel hope in the LORD, For with the LORD is mercy, with him is plenteous redemption, (Ps 130: 6-7)**

In hospitals, care facilities and sick beds all over, people are waiting. Waiting for their turn in surgery. Waiting for their medicines. Waiting for a diagnosis. Waiting for someone to answer their call light. Waiting for their breakfast. Waiting for lab results. Waiting for their pain to go away. Waiting for visitors. Waiting to be left alone. Waiting to get well. And, some of us, waiting to die.

Anxiety, fear, discouragement, anger and worry besiege us and weaken us from both without and within ourselves. Let me join in solidarity with all who are waiting.

PRAYER

Daylight is here now.
I have been waiting through the night
    In hope of the dawn.
Thank You, Lord,
    For the hope and reassurance
      it brings.
I am waiting upon

      Your blessings for this day.
        Be with me

In this place of waiting.
I know I am
    Not the only one waiting.
Give all of my caregivers and family
Whatever it is that
They need in their waiting.

I feel so vulnerable
    In my waiting –
Vulnerable to infection and fever,
    Vulnerable to worry and fear.
Protect me, Lord.
    Surround me with Your
    Protection from these evils.
Even in my waiting
  Make me an encourager
    Of faith, of hope, of peace
    And forgiveness for others
So that I, too, can be a healer of spirit and body.

I am counting on Your
    Goodness and power today,
Certain in my faith that these
    Current trials will pass and that
    In Your goodness all will be well.

AMEN.

#43 - Graciousness In the Mystery

Reflection

> ... Giving thanks always and for everything in
> the name of our Lord Jesus Christ to God the
> Father. (Eph 5:20)

I don't like mystery – it takes away my control and my sense of justice. My life is full of mystery. I often search for blame when I encounter mystery. It seems like the haze of mystery so often sends me looking for blame.

Gratitude helps me to penetrate mystery - the mystery of pain and suffering in my life.

Being a healer and being healed are both nested in and affirmed by gratitude for gifts that faith remembers and that hope expects. The habit of gratitude grounds me in times of trouble and anxiety. It stabilizes and steadies me both in times of great joy and in the times of great trouble. When I feel grateful, I am expectant of present and future graces and gifts. I pray in gratitude to God this morning.

PRAYER

Thank You God that
    I am not responsible
    For this mess!

Are You responsible?
    You are only loving,
    All loving.

There's the mystery.

Where's the gratitude that will set me free.

I feel like someone has to be responsible
    For the hurt that has been done – but –
Who is responsible for the good?
    For the love?

Love is lost
    When I choose to make myself or You
        Responsible.

For having created me and loved me,
    Thank You God.
For the place You are keeping for me in heaven,
    Thank You God.
For giving me
    The grace of gratitude this morning,
    Thank You, God.

AMEN.

#44 - Not the Way

> **For I know well the plans I have in mind for you—oracle of the Lord —plans for your welfare and not for woe, so as to give you a future of hope. (Jer 29:11)**

"Stick with the plan" is advice that is often given for what to do when in doubt. Stick with whose plan? My own or God's?

Prayer

This isn't the way
>   Today was supposed to be, Father.
>   At least, not in my plans.

And I can't figure out
>   A plan for tomorrow, Father.
>   At least not one that seems possible.

I thank You that I do not stand
>   Alone in my faith
>   Or alone in my hope.

I thank You for those who are caring for me.
Their compassion
>   Steadies my heartbeat;
Their belief in the possibility of my healing
>   Strengthens my faith.

They help me to carry my hope
When my grip on it
    Is weak and slippery.
They are angels
Whose presence and care
    Bring me the message of
        Your presence and care for me.

Despite my own plans and expectations
This is the way
    Today is supposed to be, Father,
With these caregivers who are
    My healing angels and
    Messengers of faith and hope.

Thank You, Father.
Bless them, Father,
    As You are blessing me.

AMEN.

#45 - Has God Forgotten to Be Merciful?

REFLECTION

> But this I will call to mind;
> therefore, I will hope:
> The LORD's acts of mercy are not exhausted;
> his compassion is not spent;
> They are renewed each morning — great is his
> faithfulness! (Lam 3: 21-23)

Life sometimes puts me in a state of confusion in which I do not know where to look or where to go next. When I am caught in such a state, I usually ask the question "Why". It is better that I ask the question "What".

Lord, with Your will that is always good, what is it that You are doing in my life right now?

PRAYER

Lord, when I am tempted to ask "Why?"
Grant me the grace of HOPE
    Strong enough to endure
    The pain of What I do not understand
    In my circumstances.

Grant me
        Hope that is loving enough to be a
        Peaceful presence to others
        Despite the frustration I may feel.

        Hope that is patient enough to
            Step outside of myself -
        Compassionate and calm enough
            In the midst of the frustration
            And disillusionment
            I am experiencing.

        Hope that is humble enough
            To serve You and
            Wait upon You

    In my blindness and ignorance of Your way.

AMEN

#46 - I CHOOSE TO TRUST YOU

> **Those who suffer in accord with God's will
> hand their souls over to a faithful creator as
> they do good. (1Pet 4:19)**

My life is sometimes a mystery to me, especially when there is trouble. The combination of mystery and trouble shakes my soul. There are a lot of things that I cannot know about You, God; You are a mysterious God. One thing I do know – You are good – always good. Let me trust to bury my fear and anxiety in that knowledge.

PRAYER

Lord, give me the courage, the faith,
    The hope and the humility
    Not to flee Your presence
        When I most need You,
        When I seem to face the choice
      To trust You or to rebel.

Grant me the grace to choose
    To trust You in
    Whatever mystery I am living in.

Grant me the graces of
    Courage and trust,
        Of Hope and of Faith.

Still and strengthen
    My heart and my spirit
    To endure what I do not understand
    And no-matter-what
    Trust in Your goodness.

For Your glory, heal me.
Heal all who trust in You today.

I choose to trust You.

AMEN.

#47 - Be Still and Know That I Am God

Be still and know that I am God. (Ps 46:11)

Sometimes I come to the seeming end of my abilities, the seeming end of my wits. Caught in a confusion of helplessness or fear, I forget that You are my help. I forget sometimes in my turmoil that You are indeed the source of all life and healing. Steady my heart, Lord.
Let me be still, in confidence of Your presence and power.

PRAYER

Send Your Spirit upon me, Lord,
    To remind me and
    To reassure me
    That I do not heal alone.

If I begin to panic,
    Whisper to my spirit these words:
    "Be still, and know that I am God."

Remind me throughout my day that
    You are with me:
    When I am tired,
    When I don't have as much information
        as I feel I need;
When people may seem ungrateful
        Or even angry with me;
When I am saddened for others or
        Step into my own grief;
Whenever I just don't know what to do.

Let my own heart be still in
    The knowledge that You are God,
        That in Your power,
           Your goodness,
               Your mercy and love,
                  All is in control
  I am safe.

AMEN.

#48 - FREE ME

**For just as in Adam all die, so too in Christ shall
all be brought to life. (1Cor 15:22)**

My concern for the suffering of my brothers and sisters reveals
the divine love of God that is present in my very human heart.
Healing is a setting free of the spirit and body. The ultimate
healing will be my resurrection and entrance into the Kingdom
of God. – a free citizen of heaven.

PRAYER

Bless me today, Lord.
Bless my heart.
Free me from any fear or anxiety
    That locks my heart from
    Accepting Your grace
    And. opening to You.

Bring me the peace
    That knows
        You are near,
    That knows You
        Bless me always.

Free my soul
    From any bonds or burdens that
    Prevent me from turning to You or
    Walking with You today.

Let my lips speak
    Of my love for You
    And my trust in You.

You are my God;
I am Your child.
I bless You and praise You this morning, Lord,
Trusting that You are walking with me.

AMEN.

#49 - WITHOUT MEASURE

> **Trust in the LORD with all your heart, on your
> own intelligence do not rely;
> In all your ways be mindful of him, and he will
> make straight your paths. (Prov 3:5-6)**

Trust resides in my heart. So does Peace.
My peace of heart does not come from my intellect.

A spirit of trust, of peace, comes from knowing and believing
that I am loved without measure or condition. The one who
prays to God for holiness finds grace overflowing.

PRAYER

Lord, Your ways
    Are beyond my understanding ...
    I trust myself to Your keeping today.

I entrust myself to Your safe keeping -
    Not only my own
        Living and breathing,
    But also the living and breathing of
        All whom I love.

I live and I believe because
    You have loved me into existence.

Hold me safe today
    In Your bountiful love and mercy.

Yes, I know Your love for me is
    Irrational and
        Whole-hearted.

I know that my ability to understand
    Never exceeds the measure of
    Your love for me.

This knowledge is
    Enough for today.
    Enough for my life:

You are Peace for my heart.
You are healing for my spirit and body.

Praise, glory and thanks to You!

AMEN.

#50 - CHOOSE THE GOOD TODAY

REFLECTION

> **If I take the wings of dawn and dwell beyond
> the sea, even there your hand guides me, Your
> right hand holds me fast. (Ps 139: 9-10)**

So often I fret and wonder about things to which I already know the answer.
I know that God is all-good and that He guides and cares for me always; but still sometimes I wonder a lot about my days and my safety.
Psalm 139 tells me that even should I go to the farthest, highest or deepest part of the Earth, God would be there and caring for me.

God's ways are indeed mysterious to me but of His care for me I am certain.

PRAYER

God, be with me today.
In the morning
    I ponder what this day holds.
    I ponder what You may do with today.

I wonder what may happen
    And turn to You
    For help and protection,
    For wisdom and grace.

It is Your will that
 Mysteriously and powerfully
 Makes this universe work and that will
 Hold it together
 For another twenty-four hours.

I know that it is Your will that
 Mysteriously and powerfully
  Holds my life together for another day.

You have made me in Your image.
You have given me
 A will to use today,
 A will that I can use to choose my actions
 Even though sometimes I deny that and say
 I have no choices left.

Sometimes I say that circumstance,
 Or other people,
 Or even You
 Have left me with no choices.

I do not always use my will for good.
 Forgive me, Lord, for those times.
Grant that I may choose the good today.
In thanksgiving I offer to Your service and glory
 Every word and action that I choose today.

AMEN.

Section II

Prayers For Caregivers

#51 - That I May Hear Your Voice

Reflection

**A voice said to him, Why are you here, Elijah?
(1Kings 19:13)**

Why are you here? God asked this question of Elijah when it looked like he was about to be captured and killed by Queen Jezebel. Elijah was hiding in a cave, waiting to hear God's voice. God sent a violent wind, an earthquake and fire, but His voice was in none of these. Then He sent a small, nearly silent whisper saying "Why are you here, Elijah?"

God asks us the same question every day in the voices of our patients: we have to listen carefully or we will miss it.

Prayer

Lord, bless my ears today
   - that I may hear Your voice!

Bless me
   To hear every word spoken by the lips,
   The hearts & the spirits
   Of those I care for.
That I may hear Your voice!

Bless me to hear
   The unspoken and the unsaid and
   To listen without assumption or judgment.

Bless me
    To hear with understanding,
    To hear with compassion and
    To hold myself always a gracious
        And peaceful
        Receiver of the sick and injured.
    Bless me that I may hear Your voice!

Bless me to remember that
    I am a mirror of Your presence
    When I listen to the sick
    And that the sick are also mirrors
    Of Your presence to me
    When they speak of their ills,
        That I may hear
        The whisper Your voice!

In that mirror place of listening to each other,
    May I find You present here today
    And hear
        The whisper of Your voice

AMEN.

#52 - IN THIS PLACE

Do not be saddened this day, for rejoicing in the Lord is your strength! (Neh 8:10)

Praise my loving Redeemer, who has gained for me this season of grace. Lord, create a new spirit in me. Let me walk today in newness of life. Create a new spirit in me Lord, you have brought blessings to all mankind, — bring me today to share your concern for the good of all. Healer of body and soul, cure the sickness of my spirit, so that I may grow in holiness through your constant care. Lord, create a new spirit in me. Do not let me be saddened today. Strengthen me with Your joy!

PRAYER

Come walk beside me, Lord.
    Make Your healing known,
    Make Your consolation and joy felt,
    Today, in this place.

Make my tears and my laughter be medicine.
    To brother,
    To sister,
    Today, in this place.

Giggle with me,
    When I laugh,
    And dance with me
    Today, in this place.

Lord, when I cry,
    Embrace me.
    Let my tears fall on Your shoulder.
    Today, in this place.

Lord, grace my rejoicing and my weeping
    To be peace and healing
    For any grief or fear, pain or sickness endured
    Today, in this place.

Lord, my laughter, and my tears
    Witness your own;
    May they be signs of hope and healing
    For all,
    Today, in this place.

Lord, Your presence is necessary;
    Your embrace is essential
    For my joy,
    Today, in this place!

Lord, make me to
    Rejoice with those who rejoice;
    Weep with those who weep.
    Today in this lace.

AMEN.

#53 - The Second Commandment

You shall love your neighbor as yourself. (Mk 12:31)

May my hands, my voice, my ears and my heart carry compassion and mercy to all whom I encounter today —my patients, their families, my co-workers.

I am loved. From the beginning, from before the Son came to save me, I am loved. There is no deserving the love that God gives me. That is the cause of my hope. I cannot in any way deserve the love I have received – which makes me an equal in grace to all other humans. This is what calls me to be an equal in compassion and mercy to each and every one of my brothers and sisters. Because He has loved me, I love my sisters and brothers and myself also.

PRAYER

God of Compassion and Mercy,
Free my spirit from
Any strife or anxiety
   That would strain my faith,
   Burden my hope,
   Give pause to my charity or
   Contaminate my ability to love and heal.

Send down Your Holy Spirit to
Help me to put on Christ
That I may be healer of
Both bodies and spirits.

Lord, You have already enriched my life
   With countless gifts and blessings.
For this I give You thanks and praise.

May I continue to serve
   My mission of healing
   With compassion for all and
   Reverence for everyone.

May I never forget the holiness of the work
   To which You are calling me.
After all, Lord, this is Your work, not mine.
To You be all glory, praise and honor.

AMEN!

#54 - Beacon of Your Love and Mercy

Reflection:

> **Blessed be the Lord, the God of Israel, for he has visited and brought redemption to his people. (Lk 1:68)**

How can anyone respond properly to this pronouncement? The answer is to put action to our belief! Keep a peaceful heart, proclaiming the Gospel in our life. That is what a disciple does. This is a self-fulfilling prophecy. Because He has blessed us, we are free to love. Claim your freedom!

PRAYER

Stir up Your mighty power.
　　　Lord, come to my aid today.
Make haste to help me!

True Light and
　　　Source of all light,
Hear my morning prayer.

Grace me to be
　　　Humble,
　　　Docile
　　　And aflame
　　　　　In the breath of Your Holy Spirit.
Direct my thoughts and actions
　　　By Your wisdom and love.

May I live
　　　As a beacon of
　　　Your love and mercy,
　　　...
　　　As a reflector of the Gospel light
　　　Of love and mercy
　　　...
To all in my care today.

AMEN!

#55 – Bearing the Good Fruits

Reflection

> ... so that we may be able to encourage those who are in any affliction with the encouragement with which we ourselves are encouraged by God. (2Cor 1:4)

Our concern for the suffering of our brothers and sisters reveals the divine love of God that is present in our very human hearts. Our healing work is a reminder for both healer and healed that salvation is for the whole person, for the unique mind-body-spirit creature that we are. Knowing our own experiences of suffering and pain and our own experiences of God's love and mercy, let us turn our hearts to compassionate healing. Let us bear the good fruits of compassion and mercy. Let us partner with God, following His sacred call to heal our sisters and brothers.

PRAYER

Lord, bless me for the healing
    That is to be done this day.

Let the fruit of any suffering I experience
Open my heart to compassion and mercy
        For the sick and suffering.
May the fruit of my compassion and mercy be
        That my brothers and sisters will
        Experience healing.
May Your compassion and Your mercy
    Be witnessed
    In the work of my hands,
        Mind and
            Heart.

As St. Francis prayed,
May I be an instrument of peace and hope,
Compassion and mercy to all as
I partner with You in my healing work today.

Let the fruit of any suffering I bear
Be compassion and mercy for those in my care.

Thank You. Lord, for Your call to heal.

AMEN!

#56 - Let My Every Word Prophesy Healing

Reflection

> **So shall my word be that goes forth from my mouth; It shall not return to me empty, but shall do what pleases me, achieving the end for which I sent it. (Is 55:11)**

Words are prophetic. Let your every word be a prophecy of healing and not one of discord. Prophesy peace. Your words carry power that echoes in the in the mind, body and spirit of others. To paraphrase St Paul: healing words are ... patient, kind, not jealous, not pompous, and not inflated. They are not rude and do not seek self-interest. Neither are they quick-tempered, nor do they brood over injury or rejoice over wrongdoing; rather they rejoice with the truth. Healing words hope all things.

Prayer

Lord, bless my words today.
> Bless every word
> That I speak,
> That it may bring healing.

St Francis prayed to You,
> "Lord, make me an
> Instrument of peace."
> I pray the same.

St Anthony prayed to You,
> "For the healing of many."
> I pray the same.

St Benedict prayed to You
    "Give me
    Wisdom to perceive you,
    Diligence to seek you,
    Patience to wait for you,
    Eyes to behold you."
    I pray the same.

Bless my lips to speak words
    Of kindness and compassion.
    Of hope and encouragement,
    Of respect and dignity
    Of faith and charity

Let every word I speak today
    Prophesy healing to patients, to caregivers
      And to this community.
I thank You, Lord,
    For listening to my words this morning.

AMEN!

#57 - Bless My Ears

Reflection

> **Then he looked up to heaven and groaned, and said to him, "Ephphatha!" (that is, "Be opened!") And immediately the man's ears were opened... (Mk 7:34-35)**

Our ears are connected to our head but it is to the heart that they truly belong. Others can read the state of my heart by the way I listen to them. If my ears are closed by inner discord or judgement, it is impossible for me to be a healing listener. My ears are mirrors to my heart. I desire to be a healer as powerful as Jesus was when he healed the deaf man. When I am deaf to my brother and sister, sometimes it is because my heart needs to be healed.

PRAYER

Lord, bless my ears today
  - that they may be
        Instruments of your peace.

Bless me
To hear every word spoken by the lips,
    The hearts &
        The spirits
            Of those in my care.

Bless me to hear
    The unspoken and the unsaid and
    To listen without assumption or judgment.

Bless me
    To hear with understanding,
    To hear with compassion and
    To hold myself always a
    Gracious and peaceful
    Receiver of the sick and injured.

Bless me to remember that
    I am a mirror of Your presence
    When I listen to the sick and that
The sick are also mirrors of Your presence
    To me when they speak to me of their ills.

Today I want to put on Christ's ears
And listen from my heart.

AMEN.

#58 - Incline My Heart to Your Will, O God

Reflection

> What I do, I do not understand. For I do
> not do what I want, but I do what I hate.
> (Rom 7:15)

Let us put on the heart of Christ. Like Jesus, our hearts are moved with compassion for the sick. We share a vocation to heal with Him. Everything about ourr being and our way of being seeks healing for ourselves and others. The call to heal claims our every faculty and sense. Incline our hearts to your will, O Lord.

Prayer

God our Savior,
    Hear my morning prayer.
    Keep me mindful
        In Your grace and call to be
A bearer of Light and Truth
        Every moment of today.

Grant that I may live this day
    In peace with all,
    Never rendering evil for evil, but
    Being a vessel of only charity and hope
    For the healing of this community.

Renew me this morning, Lord,
    For the sake of Your glory.
Let Your Light shine
    Through my charity.

Incline my heart according to Your will.
  Speed my steps along Your path.

I dedicate the beginning of this day
  To the glory and grace of
    Your resurrection, Lord.

May I make the whole day pleasing to You
  By my works of healing, care, compassion
    And kindness for Your people.

Teach me today to recognize
  Your presence in all whom I serve.

Incline my heart according to Your will.

AMEN.

#59 - Blessed Be My Heart

REFLECTION:

> **Rather, he emptied himself, taking the form of**
> **a slave, coming in human likeness;**
> **and found human in appearance ...**
> **(Philippians 2:7)**

Pray to God who brings salvation & healing to His people: He has come upon us bearing the same flesh as we do; yet, He is God! He is eternal, mighty and unchanging, always faithful to us every day and every moment of our lives. Blessed are You, Lord, for by Your generosity I awaken once again this morning to a living hope.

PRAYER

Grant me, Lord, a clean heart,
Renewed in Your spirit this morning,
That I may be Your good instrument of healing
For all in my care today.

Through Your Holy Spirit,
Cleanse my heart and spirit of
Any contamination and infection
As I come beside my patients.

By the power of Your Holy Spirit,
 Help me to be a good healer
  Like Your Son Jesus –

To be a merciful
And compassionate
Healer
Like Your Son Jesus.

Today, grant healing for
The sick and injured in my care,
Grant a portion of joy
To the sorrowful and lonely:
Grace and redemption to all!

Lord, let the knowledge of
Your mercy and salvation be
Healing for my heart and body.
Free me from fear and anxiety
And from any other force of evil

Blessed by You,
Fully following Your call
And imitating your Son,
I pray to serve You faithfully And be the best
servant-healer
I can be today.

AMEN!

#60 - I Carry God's Blessings in Joy

Reflection

Teach me, Lord, your way that I may walk in your truth, single-hearted and revering your name. (Ps 86:11)

Give me an undivided heart, Lord. It is difficult to remain focused when I am distracted by tiredness, frustration, ingratitude and sometimes the feeling that I cannot do enough. There are times, Lord, when I am discouraged with You, even – times when I cannot see the good You are doing. When I lose focus on Your goodness, I forget Your blessings and am blind to them. Joy is my witness to Your presence and goodness. Joy sharpens my focus. Joy is the antidote to discouragement.

PRAYER

Lord, You fill me with blessings
    Until my cup overflows,
My brothers and sisters, let us
    Carry God's blessings in joy and
    Witness to His goodness
    Especially when
        We cannot see or feel His presence.

He has gifted me
    With talents and skills for healing.
Be grateful, my soul, for these gifts and
    Share your blessings generously.
Be gracious
    And joyful
        In God's bounty.

I thank You and praise You, Lord,
    For the holiness of this work which
    You have entrusted to me.

Each morning I rise and enter the day
In joyful service to my patients.

In the midst of sometimes tiring work
    And an often-burdened heart
I serve always
    For Your great honor and glory
And for the love of my neighbor.

AMEN.

#61 - Mercy!

> Peace in place of bitterness! You have pre-
> served my life from the pit of destruction;
> Behind your back you cast all my sins.
> (Is 38:17)

This verse conjures an image of God that is one of the most consoling and hopeful for me in the Bible. There are not many things that we can count on as sure things. We are well aware tomorrow is not one of them, nor even this afternoon; but we are also wonderfully aware that two of the absolutely sure things in life are the limitless mercy of our God and the knowledge that our life does not end with our earthly death. Shakespeare wrote: *"The quality of mercy is not strained; It droppeth as the gentle rain from heaven Upon the place beneath. It is twice blest; It blesseth him that gives and him that takes." (The Merchant of Vnice, Act IV, Scene 1)* The flow of mercy between patient and caregiver is two-way. Be as ready to accept mercy as to give it.

PRAYER

I pray for our God's
    Wonderful and bountiful mercy today.

I pray, Lord, that You pour out
    Your mercy upon me and
    Upon the whole world.
May Your Divine mercy cast out
    The hardness
    And bitterness
    And skepticism
        That is in this world.
Replace them with Your healing peace.

Yes, pour out
Your Divine mercy upon me today, Lord.
Preserve my life, and
Grant me healing today
In my body, my mind and my soul.

Grace me to long for Your mercy and
    Share what I am freely given
    With others today;
Let me become the vessel that
    Pours Your mercy upon the world.

AMEN!

#62 - Compassion!

> **Blessed be the God and Father of our Lord Jesus Christ, the Father of compassion and God of all encouragement, who encourages us in our every affliction, so that we may be able to encourage those who are in any affliction with the encouragement with which we ourselves are encouraged by God (2Cor 1: 3-4)**

Jesus says: "My Father in His love sent Me as His great act of compassion for you! I have showed you the way to compassionate living, by the example of My life. As I instructed My first disciples, I counsel you to 'be merciful as your Father is merciful.'" (Luke 6:36)

PRAYER

O Lord, take away any fear and judgment
    That reside in my heart
    For they stop me from true compassion.
Help me to go beyond
    Simply being kind and gentle to
    Being an unpretentious, humble
    Presence to those suffering
    Illness, pain or misfortune.

If You can, Lord,
(Of course You can, Lord!)
Help me to do this whether my patient is
    My friend, a stranger to me or
        Even my enemy.

Lord, help me to put aside my fears and
My habitual desire to be in competition
With anyone and everyone and to be
    Willing to be humbly present with them
    In their pain and vulnerability

As You, Jesus, chose to be with us
And as You, Father,
    Chose to send Your Son Jesus
    In Your compassion for me,
    Grant me a compassionate spirit
    For my patients.

I ask Your grace to learn to be
As compassionate with others
As You are with me.

AMEN!

#63 - TGIF

REFLECTION:

**Blessed are you, and praiseworthy, O LORD,
the God of our ancestors, and glorious forever
is your name. (Dan 3:26)**

Sometimes in my relationship with God — I feel so far away
from Him or that He is so far away from me. I long for him to
be near. That is why it is good to count my blessings, even the
ones I don't know. Counting my blessings helps me through
the times that feel like separation. Counting my blessings is
not just for Fridays.

The story in Daniel of the young men cast into the furnace is
an example of the power of gratitude. Literally thrown into the
flames, they made it through the ordeal praising God for His
many blessings upon them.

PRAYER

It is good to count my blessings —
Especially on a Friday.
It is joy, relief and strength
Knowing that I have traveled the week
Under God's wing.

Sometimes I am blessed
And know it.
Sometimes I am blessed

And am not aware.
Always I must believe

I am blessed.

Lord, thank you for
    The many blessings of this week –
The people you have placed in my days,
The good work you have given me to do,
The joys and successes of each hour.

Thank You for the blessing of faith.
Thank You for the times
When I have been certain of Your presence.
Most of all, thank You for the blessing
Of Your constant love
That holds me in life.

And thank You for the love
You have given me through other people.
Thank You for the blessings I have received back
From those I have worked to heal.

I am filled with gratitude
    For Your many, many blessings, Lord,
Those I know
    And especially the uncounted ones.

AMEN.

#64 - ENCOMPASS ME, LORD

REFLECTION

> You are my shelter; you guard me from distress;
> with joyful shouts of deliverance you surround
> me. (Ps 32:7)

One of my favorite words in the Bible is *"encompass"*. It is used to describe God surrounding me on all points of the compass, protected by Him. No matter what direction I turn. I am at the center of God's grace. He is my polar North.

PRAYER

O Lord, you are the Creator and
    Sustainer of all.
Lord, You have
    Called me to life.
May the beat of my heart and
The rhythm of my breathing
    Sing gratefully
    Of Your faithful love
        Throughout this day,
        Throughout this night.

Convert my heart to be a true and loving
    Channel of Your peace:
Use it
    As an instrument of Your healing.

In need and in plenty,
In struggle and in victory,
    Your peace settles upon me,

Seeping deep into my bones,
And pours out upon
The spirits of those around me.

May I nest my heart in Yours
As sparrows build their nest
In the courtyard of Your temple.

I pray that Your good will be done
For my good,
The good of my patients
For the good of all
Who are sick and suffering,
And for Your glory.

AMEN!

#65 - THAT NONE OF US FEEL ALONE

REFLECTION:

> "Remain here and keep watch with me." He advanced a little and fell prostrate in prayer ... When he returned to his disciples he found them asleep. (Mt 26: 38,40)

Jesus was truly God and truly man. That means he experienced the full range of human emotions. He is with us in every emotion we experience.

We are not alone even though we may feel alone or abandoned; He understands our plight

PRAYER

God of Life,
    God of Mercy.
        God of healing,
            God of peace,
                Generous and loving God,

Bless me today.

I raise up to You
    My praise,
    My gratitude and
    My needs.

I serve You and my neighbor
    In my healing work.
Help me today to serve my patients

With respect,
With integrity,
With compassion and
With excellence.

May I be bound in
Solidarity with my patients,
In both their joys and their sufferings.

Listen, please, to my
Spoken and unspoken needs.

God, hear the multitude of our spirits,
Caregiver and patients,
As one voice that
None of us may feel
Alone before you.

You know our hearts.
You, know our needs.
You are ever with us.
Hear our prayer, O Lord.

AMEN.

#66 - FOR COMPASSION AND EXCELLENCE

> 'Take care of him. If you spend more than what
> I have given you, I shall repay you on my way
> back.' (Lk 10:35)

The word "generous" at its root means to be life-giving. A care-giver is generous at the root of her or his or her being,– deeply compassionate for all life! God in His love sent His son Jesus as His great act of compassion for me! He has shown the way to compassionate living, by the example of His life and also by His counsel to *"be merciful as your Father is merciful." (Luke 6:36)* The parable of the Good Samaritan gets at the essence of a good caregiver – compassion and mercy for my brothers and sisters – be they kin or stranger. We are everyone on the journey to the Holy City of God, Jerusalem.

PRAYER

God of Love, God of Life,
Help me today to be
    Life-giving
        In all I shall do and
        All I shall say and a
        Al I shall think.

Enliven my desire to answer
Your call to be
    Your hands,

        Your heart, and
            Your eyes and ears

Of compassion
In my work of tending to the sick.

In the middle of
Crisis,
Difficulty and
Simple toil,
Keep me grateful-hearted today,
Mindful of my gifts and
Thankful to have received them from You.

Give me the strengths of faith,
Of hope and
Of charity
To sweeten my work and
To share with the burdened ones in my care.

As You and I work
For the healing of my brothers and sisters today,
Scent my presence with the true
Humility,
Compassion
And Hope
Of Your Gospel.

Amen!

#67 – In Chaos

Rejoice and be glad, for your reward will be great in heaven. (Mt 5:12)

Today feels to be on the edge of Creation's chaos and the breaking-in of the Kingdom. It is a gift.
Chaos is found in mystery and suffering. Peace and joy are found in gratitude. God provides graces for each day – indeed for each hour and minute. His blessings for today await you. He has just the ones you need. Praise and thank Him for He protects us from the Chaos. Let His kingdom break in!

PRAYER

This is the day You have made, Lord.
    Filled with Your grace and protection.
        Fill it with Your guidance.
        Fill it with Your peace.
You have made this day for me.

It will be filled with mystery and suffering also:
    Lord, when we are ill and injured in body
        and spirit,
    We need You.
We need you when
    Those we love are ill or injured
    And our own spirits become disturbed
    In the chaos.

When we care for and assist
    The ill, the injured and the dying,
        Compassion and weariness
        Burden our bodies and tire our spirits.

You have made this day with blessings enough
    For all that may happen.
        I know that.
        I believe that.

I thank You and Praise You.

Yes, this is the day You have made.
        Fill it with Your grace.
        Quell the Chaos

    Bless me.
    Keep me.

I believe that this is the
    Day You have made and that
        It will be measured by
            Your kindness and grace.

AMEN.

#68 - Unless You Die to Yourself ...

> **Amen, amen, I say to you, unless a grain of wheat falls to the ground and dies, it remains just a grain of wheat; but if it dies, it produces much fruit. (Jn 12:24)**

Jesus says: "Consider My presence here today in those you serve, in those who serve with you and consider My presence in your own heart.
I call you to service to draw you out of yourself - that you may be like the grain of wheat that dies ... I am calling you to serve others as the ultimate expression of your own selfhood - that you may be like the grain of wheat that is reborn

Pause for just one moment to feel the reverence of this day and of this place – and of My calling you to be here – to this place of resurrection and new life! "

PRAYER

Lord, I offer my service to You today
  As a prayer of entreaty
      For the healing of every one of
      My patients.

  As a prayer that You
          Bring wholeness to my patients -
          The ones broken
              In body and
          The ones broken
              In spirit

  I praise You and thank You
          For all the graces You
              Supply for my service.

Take my service and any hardship or cross
    That I endure today
For my dying …
    And for my rebirth …

Refreshed in Your spirit and love,
May I be a messenger of healing today

May Thy Kingdom Come!

AMEN!

#69 - PEACE AND ALL GOOD

REFLECTION

> **Jesus came and stood in their midst and said to them, "Peace be with you." (Jn 20:19)**

Peace and all good!
Let the peace of Christ reign in your heart today.
Much like the Hawaiians use the same word of *"Aloha"* as greeting and goodbye, Saint Francis and his Friars would say *"Peace and all good"* both as they greeted each other and as they parted from one another.

If we are to heal others, it is essential for our own hearts and spirits to be at peace. So let us pray peace and all good for each other and for our patients.

PRAYER

Lord, bring peace and all good
    To this place today.
Bring peace to my heart and spirit
    That I may be a good healer and
    Be an instrument of Your grace
    For my patients and for their families.

Bring peace to all my patients
    That they may heal well.
Bring peace to the spirits of
    Those who love them
    As they stand vigil by them.

Bring peace to me, Lord,
    That my presence may be healing;
    Let my spirit be calming and encouraging.

Lord, anticipate our every need today –
    Mine and my patients' -
        With Your protecting and
            Saving grace.

I trust You, Lord.
You are the source of my peace, my healing
    And of all good.

Peace and All Good!

AMEN!

#70 - A SPIRIT OF HOPE

REFLECTION:

> **As they were going out, they met a Cyrenian named Simon; this man they pressed into service to carry his cross. (Mt 27:32)**

Dear Lord,
every day this healing work You call me to brings me to the choice to help others. Sometimes it is in simple matters; but at other times it looks like I am being asked to help carry impossible burdens; always, I am being asked to help my patients carry hope. Grant me a spirit of hope today.

PRAYER

Fill me up with Hope this morning, Lord.
Fill me with
 Strong,
 Confident and
 Contagious
 Hope:
Hope enough that I can
 Infect my patients with it and
 Make their spirits stronger.

Fill me with Hope:
Hope enough
 That I can feel my own burdens lighten,
  That my spirit may be stronger today.

When my brother and sister are too weak
        To carry their own hope,
Give me the strength to
        Be like Simon of Cyrene
And carry their hope with them.

Fill me with Your Spirit of Hope
So that with the aid of
        Your Holy Spirit,
                My spirit may be
                        Strengthened and
                        Gladdened
To bear all burdens of this day.

AMEN!

#71 - I Am Healer

> You are a refuge for me; you guard me in trouble; with songs of deliverance you surround me. (Ps 32:7)

I am a healer.

My job, my work, my call is to heal.

Yes, more than job or work, healing is my call. The God who has given life to me calls me to partner with Him in the care and healing of my brothers and sisters. No matter what my position is on the care team I have been called here as healer. I listen to broken hearts with stethoscopes and with my ears. I look inside bodies with all sorts of technology; I look into souls with my eyes. I heal with medicine, heart and spirit.

I am a healer –

and with that comes many burdens on my own spirit. I cannot help but be touched to my soul by the plight of the sick, the injured, the grieving, the oppressed and the abused. It is my hope and my faith and my caring that empowers me and graces me to be a good healer.

The daily news and events in my personal life also strain the hope and faith that are so necessary to my call and mission. I pray today that my hope and my faith be preserved and strengthened.

PRAYER

I pray this simple but powerful blessing
From the Book of Tobit:
for all of us:

At all times bless the Lord, your God, and ask him
that all your paths may be straight
and all your endeavors and plans may prosper.
...
It is the Lord
    Who gives all good things. (Tobit 4:19)

May the Lord preserve and strengthen
your hope and faith today and
make successful your work of healing.

May you be guided by His good counsel
And strengthened by His good grace.

AMEN.

#72 - GOOD STEWARDS OF GOD'S GRACE

REFLECTION:

> **As each one has received a gift, use it to serve
> one another as good stewards of God's varied
> grace... Whoever serves, let it be with the
> strength that God supplies... (1 Pet 4:10-11a)**

Let me be a Good Steward of God's varied grace. Lord,
I come to You grateful for the skills, the talents and the work
that I have.

Everything that I have is gift. Let me respond with joy and share
that joy with those around me.

PRAYER

All-powerful and ever-living God,
   Creator God,
      You are the source of lasting health.

Hear me as I ask Your loving
   Help for the sick and injured.

Restore their health.

You have gifted me
   With knowledge,
   With skills and
      With talents for healing.
Help me to use these gifts and these graces
   Well and generously.
May I be a channel of
   Healing,
      Comfort and
         Peace today.

Thank you for the blessings you have given me
   Yesterday and all the days in the past.
I am eagerly expecting the blessings
   You will pour on me today.
Because of Your faithfulness,
   I have confident hope for tomorrow.

Your faithfulness and love
   Give cause for my hope
   Through every trial and pain of my day.

Thank You, Lord.

AMEN!

#73 - LONELINESS

> **For the sake of his own great name the LORD will not abandon his people, since the LORD has decided to make you his people. (1 Sam 12:22)**

Being a caregiver is draining work. It can leave us feeling empty and alone. These feelings of isolation separate us from our patients, from God. Agitation diminishes the solidarity between patients and caregivers. It becomes difficult to be a beacon of mercy, peace and hope. It is good to recall that Jesus' name is Emmanuel – "God-With-Us".

PRAYER

God of Life,
    God of Mercy.
        God of healing,
            God of peace,
Generous and loving God,

Bless me today.
    I'm feeling alone,
    Empty.

This work,
    This healing work -
It's hard;
    I feel distant from You,
        From my patients.

I need Your help today
>To serve my patients
>>With respect, with integrity,
>>>With compassion and
>>>>With excellence
>>>>>And joy!

Fill me up'
Bind me in close solidarity
>With my patients.
Let this feeling of loneliness
>Not drain me of compassion.

Be with me; Lord.
Let me know Your presence.

Loving God, Living God,
May the good works You accomplish
In me and through me today
Bring healing and life to
>My sisters and brothers,
And give glory, honor and praise to You.

AMEN!

#74 - FREEDOM

> "with a firm reliance on the protection of
> divine Providence, we mutually pledge to each
> other our Lives, our Fortunes and our sacred
> Honor." (Concluding phrase of the Declaration
> of Independence)

Guided by these words, our forefathers declared their freedom.
Making the same pledge to God, we declare our own freedom
from the tyrannies of worry, anxiety, fear and self-interest.

PRAYER

O God of Power and Strength,
    God of Faithfulness and Hope,
        God of Mercy and Love.
As I do every day of my life,
    I am counting on You
    To give me my daily bread,
    To nourish
        And to grace
        My body and spirit
            For today's Journey of service.
I pledge myself to be reverent with all and
    Reverent for the work
        You give my hands today.
I pledge to be truthful with all,
    Respecting their dignity.
I pledge to be compassionate towards all
    And with myself.
Let the example of Your own

Unfailing kindness and mercy
Guide me in this.
I pledge to be the
Most excellent healer that I can be,
Conscientious to give my very best
As I accomplish
Both the simple and difficult
Works of today
Both the menial and extraordinary
Tasks of today.

I pledge these things knowing that
Under Your power and might
I am free to choose the good.

Lord, give me today my daily bread,
My daily grace.
Allow me the honor of
Serving You and the sick.

I pray this with the faith and hope of
A heart grateful
For the many blessings with which
You have already nourished me.

AMEN.

#75 - God of Healing - God of Life.

> **And one of them, realizing he had been healed, returned, glorifying God in a loud voice. (Lk 17:15)**

The Lord is a God of healing. He is constantly and faithfully blessing me to life. How often am I oblivious to His blessings? Practicing gratitude makes me a better, more effective, healer. Joy releases the grace within me.

Prayer

I adore you and praise You.
　　I thank You for
　　　　Your many blessings.

Give me strength, wisdom and knowledge
That I may take the blessings and graces
You give me and
　　　　Use them to be a good healer for
　　　　　　The ones in my care today.

Be present here, Lord.
　　　　Walk with me - at my side.
Send Your holy angels to
　　　　Guide me and guard me.

Lord, I am forgetful and
Sometimes not very gracious;
Never let me begrudge my service
Nor forget my blessings
    Because of
        Tiredness,
            Disappointment or
                Selfishness.

When I am healed,
When You use me for the healing of others,
Make my spirit sparkle with gratitude and joy:
Remind me to give you thanks and praise.

For Your honor, glory and praise and
for the good of Your people,
    Let me share with joy
    Every blessing that I receive today.

AMEN!

#76 - GOOD LISTENING

REFLECTION

"Listening can be a greater service than speaking." (Eric Bonhoeffer)

Listening is an important part of our healing work. When we listen attentively to our patients and to each other, we become imitators of God who attends to all of our needs.

Respectful listening is a way to give dignity. Heartfelt listening is a way to express compassion.

Deep and attentive listening is a way to discover paths of healing that we might otherwise miss in our busy-care of our patients.

Good listening is good healing.

I pray that God teach me to listen well and thus be a better healer.

PRAYER

Teach me to listen, O God
    With a heart that
        loves like Yours,
    With a heart that
        Is humble like Yours and
    With a heart that
        Is full of hope and faithfulness.

Teach me to listen compassionately
To the whispers, pleas and cries of my patients
        When they may be Hopeless,
        Discouraged, or confused.
When they hope for their healing,
        Let me hope with them.

Let my listening be
　　Encouragement and strength for them.

Teach me to listen, O God my Creator,
　　For Your voice –
　　　　In busyness and in boredom,
　　　　In certainty and in doubt,
　　　　In noise and in silence.

Teach me to listen, O Creator God,
　　To myself also.
Help me to be less afraid to trust
　　The voice inside.
Where I can hear Your Holy Spirit
Whispering, in the language of
Healing, encouragement, patience,
　　Hope and wisdom.

Grace me, Lord, to be a good listener
　　And a good healer today.

AMEN.

#77 – Grant Healing for My Every Illness

REFLECTION

> **Jesus went around to all the towns and villages, teaching in their synagogues, proclaiming the gospel of the kingdom, and curing every disease and illness. (Mt 9:35)**

Matthew 11:5 further tells us "... the blind regain their sight, the lame walk, lepers are cleansed, the deaf hear, the dead are raised, and the poor have the good news proclaimed to them." Jesus came to heal.
It should be no surprise that He calls us to do the same. Let us pray for our patients, pray for the grace of their healing.

PRAYER

You, Lord, are the great Healer,
The Most Compassionate, and the
        Most Powerful of all healers.
Help me today to bring Your
        healing to my patients.
Grant healing for their every illness and
        injury of body and spirit.

Grant them wisdom and peace
To see their way through
    All the choices,
        All the uncertainties and
            All the The fears
                That they may face today.

Your blessings,
> Which I sometimes cannot see,
> Are the pledge of Your love for me
> And the sign of my safety.

Be with me in my every trial.
Grant me confidence of
> Your presence.

I am Your child.
You are my good Father.

Bless and keep my patients today, Lord.
Shine Your face upon them.
> Be gracious to them.
Grant in Your goodness
That they may live today
> In the peace
> > Of Faith and
> > > Of Hope.

AMEN!

#78 - Renew Me, Lord

Then the King will say to those on his right, 'Come, you who are blessed by my Father; Take your inheritance, the kingdom prepared for you since the creation of the world.' (Mt 25:34)

Sometimes we lose the freshness of our zeal for healing; we fall victim to burnout. Let us pray for passion in our healing. Pray that our spirits are renewed in their awareness of the love that surrounds us. Love is the river from which our healing flows. Our passion preaches God's loving presence. When our spirits become contagious with sweet hope and faith, we become powerful healers.

PRAYER

Renew me, Lord,
    That I may be the good healer
        You call me to be.
Refresh me in my healing service.

Open my spirit to
Your love that encompasses me
    That I may be a powerful healer.

Let me bear the good news of healing
    In my heart and
        Share this good news of the Gospel
          With the sick,
            The injured and the grieving.

Let my every action today preach
    Your loving presence
        Here among us.
Let my spirit be contagious
    With sweet hope
        And faith.

Use me, Lord, as a vessel
    To pour out Your healing Spirit
        Upon my patients today.
Refresh in my soul
    The gifts of life and love that
        You have planted in me
That I may be a powerful healer, today.

AMEN!

#79 - My Cup Overflows

**Indeed goodness and mercy will pursue me all
the days of my life. (Ps 23:6)**

When our service is tinged with goodness and mercy, abundant graces pour out upon our patients. In their lives filled with crisis, difficulty and pain, goodness and mercy are a beacon of hope, a balm of healing to carry the graces of vitality and health to our patients. We must put on the true humility of the Gospel.

PRAYER

Let my cup overflow
    With the graces of mercy,
        Hope
            And charity;
May these graces
    Pour out upon my patients and
        Sweeten my work.

Enliven my desire to care
    For those who come to me
        To be healed.
In the middle of crisis,
    Difficulty and
        Simple toil,
    Keep me grateful-hearted,

Mindful of my gifts
And thankful
To have received them from You.

As You and I work for
The healing of my brothers and sisters
Scent my presence with
The true humility and
Compassion of Your Gospel.

Loving God, Living God,
May the good works You accomplish
In me and through me today
Bring healing and life to Your people and
Show praise, honor and glory to You.

AMEN.

#80 - Praise and Thanksgiving

Reflection

Give thanks unto the Lord; for he is good: because his mercy endures forever. (Ps 118:1)

Of all the tools, instruments and disciplines of healing that we employ, the habitual practice of encouragement, hope, faith and peaceful presence are bedrock; and underlying these is a grateful spirit. God is good all the time – all the time God is good.

Mercy is like the flowers on the bedside table that express love and joy and soften our hearts to be grateful.

Gratitude is the ointment that opens our heart.

Gratitude is the catalyst of healing.

Prayer

God of Healing,
God of Mercy and Might,

I praise you for your great glory.
You have enriched my life with many gifts.
    I celebrate my many blessings.
        I give you thanks.

Please continue to pour
    Your grace upon me, Lord,
So that I may use well

These skills and talents for healing
With which You have gifted me.

Use me as Your instrument
    Of encouragement,
    Of hope,
    Of faith
    And of peace
    For my patients and their families.

May Your kingdom come on earth today
    As it is in heaven.

I ask this from You my loving Father
    In the name of Your Son,
    My Lord and brother Jesus Christ.

AMEN!

#81 - Prayer on a Wednesday Morning

Reflection

> **When Jesus saw her weeping and the Jews
> who had come with her weeping, he became
> perturbed and deeply troubled, and said,
> "Where have you laid him?" They said to him,
> "Sir, come and see."
> And Jesus wept. (Jn 11: 33-35)**

"Perturbed and deeply troubled" are feelings that caregivers know well. Jesus was brought to tears, as I so often am in my ministry. I encounter almost daily mysteries that I don't understand. Often I cry over them.

In those same mysteries I also find hope. Even Jesus wept: I am not alone in my tears.

Prayer

God of mystery and might,
God of hope,
God of life,
      Hear my prayer.
Come to my assistance.
Help me as I go about
      My work of healing and service.

Open my heart to
      Sing Your praises
Let my lips
      Speak of Your goodness.
Guide my thoughts, my words and my actions

Through the labyrinth of today.
Sustain my faith;
Sustain my hope
Through every joy
And sorrow,
Every challenge
And difficulty.

Be present to me, Lord,
As I strive to be patient,
Consoling
And encouraging.
Let every word and action of mine today be healing ones.
Make me a sign of
Hope,
Healing
And love
For others
In the middle of
The mysteries of
Suffering,
Illness and
Pain.

AMEN.

#82 - A Prayer for All Caregivers

Reflection

'Come, you who are blessed by my Father. Inherit the kingdom prepared for you from the foundation of the world.' (Mt 25:34)

Sometimes it seems like there is no reward – only weariness and grief – for the care I give.
It can be a short distance between burning passion and burning out. I pray today for all caregivers that they persevere and know they will be rewarded.
Refresh our spirits and bodies that we may heal the many bodies and spirits of our patients.

Prayer

Good and gracious God,
I ask Your blessing and protection
    For all Care Givers.
We daily and humbly partner with You and each other
    In answer to Your holy call to
    Heal and bless.

Guide us with wisdom;
Sustain us in trials and weariness;
Strengthen us in Hope and Charity
    Through all the difficulties we may Encounter today.

When we need a moment of respite,
Let us lean on Your shoulders
>To rest a moment,
>To share a hug or
>To leave a tear.

May we be a blessing
>To our patients,
>To each other and
>To this community.

Relieve, Lord, our weariness
>As we give care;
Grace us to witness and share
>The Hope You supply
>>For the healing and
>>The easing of the Burdens
>>Of all those we care for.

Today, may Your blessings flow
>Through our hearts and hands
For the glory of Your Name, for our good
And for the healing of all Your holy people.

AMEN.

#83 - HEAL THE HEALER

> **"It was not you who chose me, but I who chose you and appointed you to go and bear fruit that will remain, so that whatever you ask the Father in my name he may give you." (Jn 15:16)**

St. Irenaeus wrote:
"This is the glory of man: to persevere and remain in the service of God. For this reason, the Lord told his disciples: 'You did not choose Me but I chose you.'"

Every shift that I work begins with *"Here I am, Lord"*. He has chosen me, called me, to this work of healing. In order to sustain, in order to persevere, I must constantly be renewed and healed. I pray for my own healing today

PRAYER

O God of Healing, help me to be a good healer.
O God of Healing, help me to be healed.

Whether I am seeking today
    To heal or
    To be healed,
    Faith, Hope and charity are
    Necessary to me.

Rejuvenate my spirit with
    An increase of faith and hope
        That I may become a more
        Intentional healer.

Heal my relationships with You,
>With others and with my own self.
Rid my spirit of those things that
>Impede my ability to heal.
Heal my body and spirit of all things that
>Make me a hesitant healer.

May I help the sick to carry their own hope
>When they are weakened
>By pain of body and spirit.

O Lord, my healer,
I have been healed through Your suffering.
You have restored me to wholeness
>By Your cross and resurrection.
Your great love and mercy have healed me.
Bless me, Lord.
O God of Healing,
>Continue to heal me today.
>That I may better serve You and
>My brothers and sisters.

AMEN!

#84 - Rest Your Hand Upon Me Today

Reflection

Behind and before you encircle me and rest your hand upon me. (Ps 139:5)

Our healing work brings the gift of affirmation of the ways of our God Who calls each of us His "Beloved".
Guide me in Your ways today, O Lord, for You are my God and I am Your Beloved One.
Rest Your hand upon me today.

Prayer

May my life be a hymn of praise to You, O God, and my work today a song of gratitude.

May Your glory shine forth in my every
    Action and word –
    In what I do and in
        What I Choose to
        Refrain from doing;
    In what I say and in
        What I Choose to
        Refrain from saying.

Strengthen me in my love of You
    And of neighbor;
Root and form me in Gospel
    Compassion and mercy.

Use my heart; use my mind, my soul and my ears, eyes and hands
    That Your people may be healed
    That they may know Your abundant
        Love,
            Compassion
                And mercy.

God of all Goodness,
    May I be a healer who brings to life
    All the best that is in myself
    And in my neighbor;

May I bring others
    To see the goodness that
        You have created in them
    And to know They truly are
        Your Beloved Ones,
            Your treasured ones.

Glory to You, God of all peoples.
You are my Creator and Healer.
I am Your Beloved.
Rest Your hand upon me today, Lord.

AMEN!

#85 - THE WEB OF LIFE

> **"Humans did not weave the web of life – we each are merely a strand in it. Whatever we do to the web, we do to ourselves and to each other." (Chief Seattle of the Duwamish)**

The web of life is God's creation.
When one of us suffers it affects us all.
When one of us is healed, we all share in that healing.

PRAYER

And so, Lord God, I give You
   All I do today,
      All my thoughts,
      All my words,
      All my deeds
And I ask that You bless them to be healing.
   For Your glory,
   For my benefit,
   And the benefit of all Your people.
      For we are Your people, O God.

We are the people You have made.
You are our shepherd; we are Your flock.

Tend to us today, Lord and
   Help us to tend to each other.
Grant us faith, hope and charity
   Sufficient for all.

AMEN.

#86 - A Healer's Prayer

> **"Cure the sick and say to them, 'The kingdom
> of God is at hand for you.'" (Lk 10:9)**

Jesus instructed His disciples to share the good news of salvation with the sick – to be prophets of healing.
My presence to the sick, my touch, my listening, my compassion, are prophetic of the Kingdom. My calling is to be Prophet of Healing.

PRAYER

Lord,
You have called me to this healing work
So that I may be
    Blessing
        To my brothers and sisters
        Who come to me to be healed.

Make me a prophet of their healing
    When they
        Need my presence,
        Need my touch,
        Need my ears,
        Need my heart,

Give me a
        Soothing word to speak to them,
        A word that is an
        Ointment of peace;
    A word that is prophetic of God's love.

Give me these blessings:
    Joy and laughter to share with
        Weary souls
    And compassion for
        The broken ones.

I pray to have gentle, healing hands
    For those in my care;
May I be blessing to those who come to me.
May I be blessing to their families.

May I be blessing to those with whom I work.
May I be blessing and prophet.
      For Your glory
      And the good of my patients.

AMEN!

#87 - STRENGTH TO HEAL

For he commands his angels with regard to you, to guard you wherever you go. (Ps 91:11)

"Angel of God, my guardian dear, to whom God's love commends me here..." This is a prayer I learned when I was a child. It is a prayer that in its beautiful simplicity I can pray as an adult, too. I am charmed by the idea that we each have our own personal guardian. Angels are powerful; angels are messengers of hope.

Among the stories of angels in scripture is the account of the Angel of God protecting the young men in the furnace in the book of Daniel. Gabriel was the great messenger of God. Raphael is the patron saint of Healers. With the help of the angels, we practice powerful medicine and are messengers of God's love to those we care for.

PRAYER

Angel of God,
Be with me today as I work to heal the sick.
I ask you
To inspire me,
To strengthen me,
To bring me patience, wisdom, courage,
Faith, hope and charity for my healing work
As I work to
Heal bodies and spirits. and
To Soothe, comfort, console
And cure the sick.
Help me to break today the bonds that
Bind body, mind and spirit.

Use my hands, use my heart,
Use my hope, my faith and my love
As channels of God's grace
For renewing, refreshing and healing
        Those whom I touch today.

Come Holy Angels
To guide and guard me,
To comfort, console and strengthen me,
        To rejoice with me and to cry with me.

Michael, Gabriel, Raphael,
Summon all the holy Angels
        To protect me and my patients today.

AMEN.

#88 - THE MYSTERY OF SUFFERING

REFLECTION

> He said: "The Son of Man must suffer greatly
> and be rejected by the elders, the chief priests,
> and the scribes, and be killed and on the third
> day be raised." (Lk 9:22)

It is futile to try to make meaning of suffering using only the power of our own human knowledge and intellect. Suffering is a mystery greater than our ability to understand.

We encounter suffering daily in our own lives and in those whom we care for. It usually seems to be meaningless.

What do we do with that? Stand on what we know: God's will is always good and His love is constant. These are the facts of our faith. Any attempt to understand the mystery of suffering must be set within these facts.

Only in the suffering and death that Jesus shares with us can I glimpse the magnitude of God's love for me.

I can stand in His love without understanding it.

Jesus himself entered the mystery of suffering in His own passion and death. "Christians must lean on the cross of Christ just as travelers lean on a staff when they begin a long journey. They must have the passion of Christ deeply imbedded in their minds and hearts; because only from it can they derive peace, grace, and truth." (Quote from St Anthony of Padua)

PRAYER

I do not understand, Lord,
What is happening.

I know that it is not necessary that I understand,
    Only that I love.
But, still I crave to understand.
    I can carry this hurt
        Only in my faith
        In Your goodness and
        Of Your Love for me.
Be my strength in
    This place of sickness and suffering.
Console me, Lord, and
    Those I care for
        In Your love.
I trust You.

Amen.

#89 - Partnering With God

> God blessed them and God said to them: be
> fertile and multiply; fill the earth and subdue
> it. Have dominion over the fish of the sea, the
> birds of the air, and all the living things that
> crawl on the earth. (Gen 1:28)

You have taught us from the beginning scriptures of Genesis
that You charge all of us with the care of Creation and of
each other.

In the parable of the Good Samaritan and in many other places
in scripture, You taught us again and again that we are to care
for each other. Lord, You have honored me by calling me to
be healer. I am graced to partner with You in my ministry
of healing.

PRAYER

You are the Great Creator of all;
    The Giver of All Blessings.
At Your call,
    I will tend to Your creation today,
        Gratefully and joyfully
            Offering my service of healing.

I commit my talents and skills today
    To heal and strengthen
    My patients and their families.

Bless me with Your gifts of
    Wisdom and
    Hope.
Give me patience when I am tired,
    Strength when I am weak,
    And the grace of hospitality
        For every encounter.

Loving God,
Lay Your healing hands upon me now.

Let me walk always in Your love.
Let my every action and word today
    Bring healing
    And give glory, honor and praise to You,
    My loving God.

AMEN!

#90 - Give Me Courage

Reflection

> **He guides me along right paths for the sake of his name. (Ps 23:3)**

There are many obstacles that I need to push through or to get around on my daily path of service. I often need a guide along the way who will both protect and strengthen me.

When there are choices before me I need a guide who will show me the way. I need a guide who will encourage me through toil, tiredness and fear and grief. I need a guide who is a shepherd. I pray for perseverance and courage on the hard trail.

Prayer

O God of Power, Strength,
    Faithfulness and Hope,
You have given me Your protection
    Through the night.
Now I ask You to
    Shepherd me through this day.

Give me fortitude for difficult tasks and
Patience for difficult relationships.
Walk this day at my side, Lord.
With Your rod and Your staff,
    Give me courage!

Protect and heal my spirit from any trials of
    Temptation, worry, pain, doubt or fear
    I might face today.

Restore my strength when
    I tire from toil, startle from pain or
    Falter in anxiety.
Do not let my faith, hope or charity be
    Diminished by any burden of this day.

I am Your child.
    You have given me life.
Shepherd me today.
    Guide me along the right path
        For the sake of Your Name.

AMEN.

#91 - A Closer Walk with Him Today

REFLECTION

> **Rejoice with those who rejoice; weep with those who weep. (Rom 12:15)**

"My Child," Jesus says, "If today you should have tears, let them fall on My shoulder. If today you have reason to dance, take My hand and we shall laugh together! I shall walk this day with you. Side-by-side, we shall heal and be healed today.
You are not alone with either your tears or with your joy! I shall tend to your heart.

I wept when my friend Lazarus was buried in the tomb and I rejoiced when he came forth! When you weep, I shall weep with you: when you laugh, I shall rejoice with you."

PRAYER

Today, Lord, in my healing work,
    Let my tears and my laughter be
        Medicine
        To my patients and
        To my companions

When I laugh today, Lord,
    Dance with me.

When I cry today, Lord,
    May Yours be the shoulders
    my tears fall on.

I so depend on
    Your presence and
    Your embrace
        To make it through the day.

Let me find your presence
        In both the laughter and the tears
        That we share today,
        And be healed by them.

I pray for health and healing in Your Holy Name.

AMEN.

#92 - Bless You, All Nurses and Caregivers!

Reflection

> Are they not all ministering spirits sent to serve, for the sake of those who are to inherit salvation? (Heb 1:14)

Your work is holy. You have been chosen and called to be a ministering spirit. Your service is divinely commissioned. May you be blessed as you bless others.

PRAYER

Blessed be your hands
    That have touched and healed
    The many bodies
    Brought to you sick,
        Wounded,
            Infected and
                Fevered.

Blessed be your ears
    That have heard and healed
    Countless souls
    Brought to you sick with fear
    And pain, grief and loneliness.

Blessed be your eyes
    That have seen and healed the minds,
    The bodies and the spirits
        Of the many tearful Patients
        And families
        Who have received Your care.

Most Blessed be your hearts
    When you have stayed faithfully
    Beside those whose bodies
    You could not heal.

You are angels among us.
We give thanks to God for you
    And ask His blessing upon you.

AMEN.

#93 - FOR REVERENCE

**Then God said: Let us make human beings in
our image, after our likeness. (Gen 1:26)**

Of all of God's creation, only humans did He make in His image
and likeness. We are special, unique; each of us. God has given
us a dignity that is even above the angels. Let us pray for rev-
erence today – reverence for ourselves, for one another, for
our patients and their families, for all of creation.

Lord, You are the Creator and giver of all life. When I touch my
patients, I am touching Your holy creation; I am touching Your
image and likeness.

PRAYER

Lord, You have made us in Your image,
>Each of us beautiful and wonderful,
>Each of us fashioned in Your image.

Whether we are cook, engineer, doctor,
>Nurse, technician, manager,
>Administrator, or patient,
>>We each have received
>>>Life from You –
>>>A holy gift.

Help us today to be mindful to
>Treat each other with reverence,
>>To remember that
>>>You have made us to be Your people,

That You have made each and
Every one of us
In Your likeness.

It is sometimes difficult for me
To see that likeness;
And it is sometimes difficult for me
To show that likeness.

Lord, help me with Your grace today
That I may keep reverence for Your
Presence in all whom You have created.

May my efforts to be reverent
In all my actions today
Be encouragement for others.
Bring healing
For every patient I care for and
Comfort for their families.

AMEN.

#94 - HOLY HEALING

Summon again, O God, your power, the divine power you once showed for us. (Ps 68: 29)

Miracles happen every day but we don't always see them. "Do you believe in miracles?" is a question that is commonly asked around here.

Whether or not we see a miracle depends on our state of heart. Every healing is worked by the grace of God. Sometimes the healing happens in body and spirit and sometimes only in the spirit; in either case it is by the grace of God and our faith. Let us pray for the miracle of healing to happen here today.

PRAYER

O Lord, You have made me
    And know me intimately.
Indeed, You have made all of creation
    And know its every working.

Not only are You the Creator of life, but
    You are also the Sustainer
        With knowledge, power and wisdom
            Beyond my understanding.

Everything about You, Father, is
    Beyond my comprehension –
        The deepness of Your love for me,
        The wideness of Your mercy and
        The endless measure of

Your compassion and care for me.

If to be holy means to be like You, God,
   Then make me holy today;
   Make me a sustainer of life,
   Make me to be a good healer;
   Make me a powerful and wise healer.
   Make me a holy healer.

Most of all
   Make me to imitate
   Your love, your mercy and your compassion
   As I care for and heal the bodies and spirits
   Of those who come to me for healing today.

AMEN.

#95 - For the Healing You Will Do Among Us

You shall serve the LORD, your God; then he will bless your food and drink, and I will remove sickness from your midst. (Ex 23:25)

God pledges our health.
We must claim His pledge in our hearts.
He is always at work among us. Every act of His will is good – for our health of body and spirit. What is evil does not come from Him. Let us serve Him today as He works His mercy among us.

God is good – all the time.
All the time God is good.

PRAYER

Loving God, Creator God,
I thank you for this new day –
     This new day that is Your gift to me.

I thank You for Your faithfulness –
     For yet another sunrise,
     For Your day-after-day walk beside me and
     For Your night-after-night watch over me.

You are true to me
     Like a spouse in a marriage vow –
          In good times and in bad,
               Always good.

Help me to be true to You
  In good times and in bad also.

Tend to the needs of my heart
  And the desires of my spirit.
  Strengthen both heart and spirit,
  Bathing them in hope
  And encouragement.

Lord, I pray to You for the healing of the sick,
  For the comforting of their pain and sorrow.
    Bring Your grace and help
    To restore their spirits and bodies.

Grace me to use my skills and talents,
  My medicines, knowledge and wisdom
  For the healing of my sick and injured
  Brothers and sisters.

Make Your mercy, love and glory known
  Through my service.

AMEN!

#96 - BLESS EVERY WORD I SPEAK

REFLECTION

> The babble of some people is like sword
> thrusts, but the tongue of the wise is healing.
> (Prov 12:18)

I pray to be mindful of my words today.
Words can curse.
Words can bless.
Words can heal.
The tongue of the wise brings healing.

PRAYER

Lord, bless my words today.
Bless every word that I speak,
　　That it may bring healing.

Bless my lips to speak words
　　Of kindness and compassion.
　　Of hope and encouragement,
　　Of respect and dignity
　　Of faith and charity"

Let the words I speak here today
　　Bring healing
　　　　To patients,
　　　　To caregivers and
　　　　To this community.

I thank You, Lord, for listening
　　To my words this morning.

AMEN.

#97 - Make Me Whole, Lord

Reflection

> **You formed my inmost being; you knit me in**
> **my mother's womb. I praise you, because I am**
> **wonderfully made; wonderful are your works!**
> **(Ps 139: 13-14)**

The Lord has made me according to His divine design – wonderfully! He knit me together body, mind and soul – without seam! If one gets out of order, the others quickly follow suit. When all are in tune, I am in a state of wholeness and healthiness!

Lord, You call me by my human presence to bring Your divine presence to my patients today.
O God, awaken me to Your presence this morning.

Prayer

Together, Lord, let us bring
    Wholeness and
    Healing
    To this place today.

Lord You have made me wonderfully
    Both body and spirit –
So amazingly that my body can be
        Infected by an illness in my soul. -
      A trembling, fearful, grieving
          Or broken heart can
    Bring illness to my body.

So amazingly
    Have You made me body and spirit that
        My soul is pierced by pain
            And illness in my body:
    A broken bone, a cancer,
        A failing liver can
        Bring fear, regrets or grief
            To my heart and soul.

Illness, accident, fear, regrets and
    Damaged relationships
        Assault my whole self –
        Body and Spirit.

And so I pray with expectant hope this morning
        For myself and for all caregivers;
I pray for healing of
        Whatever afflicts our souls
        And our bodies.
I ask for healing of our whole selves.

Make us whole today, Lord.
Make us wholly Yours!
Make us holy.

AMEN.

#98 - FILL THIS DAY WITH HOPE, LORD

REFLECTION

May the God of hope fill you with all joy and peace in believing, so that you may abound in hope by the power of the Holy Spirit. (Rom 15:13)

Blessings pour down upon me every day. My work is constantly filled with blessings given and blessings received. Without them, I would lose hope; without hope, I would be a poor healer. I pray for God's blessing today.

PRAYER

This is the day You have made, Lord.
    Fill it with Your grace.
    Fill it with Your protection
    Fill it with Your guidance.
    Fill it with Your peace
    Fill it with Your hope.

Let Your blessings overflow in Hope
    From me to my patients
    And from them to me.

Lord, when I am ill and injured
    In body and spirit,
        I need You.

I need you:
> When my own spirit
>> Becomes disturbed.
> When those I love
>> Are ill or injured,

When I care for and assist the ill and injured,
> Compassion and weariness tire
> Both my body and my spirit.

I beg Your blessings today:
> For the restoration
>> Of wholeness to the bodies
>> Of my patients.
> Grant relief to the spirits
>> Of the ones who worry and grieve.

This is the day You have made.
Fill it with Your grace;
> Fill it with hope.

AMEN.

#99 - A Journey of Service

REFLECTION

Then the LORD said to Moses: I am going to rain down bread from heaven for you. (Ex 16:4)

For forty years God sustained the Israelites with a supply of manna – their daily bread - on their desert journey.
Each day is a journey for me - a journey on which I care for the sick and the injured ones.

God faithfully supplies me with my daily bread, my daily portion of graces. Let me use these graces to journey well – being a reverent, truthful, compassionate and excellent healer. I can travel in peace knowing that my every need will be supplied.

PRAYER

O God of Power and Strength,
God of Faithfulness and Hope,
God of Mercy and Love.

As I do every day of my life,
I am counting on You again today
To give me my daily bread,
To nourish me and
To grace me in body and spirit
For today's journey of service.

I pledge to be reverent with others and
          Reverent for the work
                You give my hands and heart today.

I pledge to be compassionate with others
    And with myself.
I pledge to be the most excellent healer
   That I can be,
    Conscientious to give my very best
      As I accomplish both the
      Simple and the difficult,
      the menial and
      The extraordinary tasks of today.

The example of Your own unfailing
    Kindness and mercy
    Guides me in this.

Lord, give me today my daily bread,
    My daily grace.
Allow me the honor of serving You
    And my neighbor today
      On this my journey of service.

AMEN.

#100 - Places of Waiting

Reflection

> Wait for the LORD, take courage; be stout-hearted, wait for the LORD! (Ps 27:14)

There are many beginnings in life and a lot of waiting. There are endings, too. Endings have their time of waiting also. Both beginnings and endings can be places of satisfaction, excitement, regret, suspense, grief or even fear. Our days are filled with these places of waiting.

Be with us today, Lord.
I pray for Your presence with me, Lord, in all the beginnings and in all the endings and in all the waiting places of this day.

PRAYER

Your name is Emmanuel, *"God-With-Us"*.
Whether it be a time of anticipation or dread,
    Regret or joy,
        You are *"God-with-Us"*,
        "God-With-Me"!

Come into my heart, Lord,
    That I may carry You with me
    Through all the
        Beginnings,
            Endings and
                Waiting places.

God, be with me this day
    In all my needs and hurts.

Be with me that I may carry You to others
    Who need Your presence,
    Who wait for healing.

I thank You for being born among us,
For being with us
    In the beginnings,
    The waitings,
    The struggles,
    The victories
    And the endings that may happen today.

I thank You and I praise You, Lord,
For Your presence with me.

AMEN.

ABOUT THE AUTHOR

David Rapp is a retired hospital chaplain and an active Deacon in the Archdiocese of Seattle. He completed his Clinical Pastoral Education at Saint Joseph Medical Center in Tacoma, Washingon. He received his Masters in Pastoral Studies from Seattle University and post-graduate certificates in Pastoral Leadership and Spiritual Direction. He is board-certified by the National Association of Catholic Chaplains. He is an avid writer and a painter.

THEME INDEX:

POSTSCRIPT

This book is meant for healing – for patients and for those who care for them. For seventeen years I have been a hospital chaplain and have had many experiences of the power of prayer in the lives of patients and their caregivers. These prayers and thoughts are a compilation of some of the prayers and conversations that I have had with patients and their nurses, doctors and caregivers. I have been blessed by them all. I have observed the bonds of compassion and faith that form between patients and their caregivers. Prayer is a language of healing for both. This book is written in that language.

"The flesh is weak" is the description Jesus gave of his disciples in the garden of Gethsemane when they were emotionally and physically overcome as they witnessed his suffering. "The *spirit is willing"* is the connecting thread of the reflections and prayers in this book. Jesus knows our suffering. Because he was fully human as well as fully divine, he experienced pain and suffering exactly as we do. There is nothing we experience that he has not. Because of that, Jesus is always present and ever compassionate with us in our suffering: we are never alone. There are times when it helps to place myself beside Jesus in the Garden of Gethsemane when I pray. When I do this, I am blessed with the assurance that I am not alone and am fortified against feelings of isolation. These prayers and thoughts are written for those times when the flesh is weak – are written to encourage the spirit.

This book promotes your healing. Expect healing because God is good all the time – all the time God is good. Your healing may be in body or in mind or in spirit or in all three.

Prayers and Thoughts is written for the acutely ill, the chronically ill, the terminally ill, for those recovering from surgery or accident and for their caregivers. These reflections and prayers are for anyone who is being stressed by or grieving their illness or that of someone they are caring for. They are prayers of consolation, encouragement and empowerment for the spirit.

What is healing? Becoming whole is becoming healthy and holy. We are healthy when we are whole. The whole self is made up of body, mind and spirit. Healing is the restoration of peace, of right order, to any of these three parts of ourselves. The healing of one contributes to the healing of the others and thus the healing of the whole self.

I once knocked on the door of a suicidal woman and she challenged me with the question: *"Who sent you? God? Or "them"?* My answer could only be *"God!"* Helping others to carry their faith and their hope when the flesh is weak is my calling. God has sent me to do this work. Hebrews 3:13 tells us to *"encourage one another daily"*. This has been my mantra for the seventeen years that I have served as a hospital chaplain. It has been the motivation for me to write this book -to encourage you in your healing and in your caregiving.

Whether we are caregivers by profession or by pledge, it is a holy work that we do. It is a partnering and a covenanting relationship. We walk with God: we walk with our patient: we walk with other caregivers. It does not matter whether the caregiver has some kind of specialized care training, certificate, an advanced nursing degree or even an MD – the work is not theirs. The work of healing, of making whole, is really

God's work, not our own. When we pledge our care to anyone, whether they be stranger or spouse, parent, child, sibling or anyone else, we are partnering with God for their healing. There are three partners, three pilgrims, on the journey of the sick: God, the sick person and the caregiver. Prayer and compassion are the arteries that connect and heal them.

Every caregiver and every patient is a minister of healing to themselves and to the other.

Every caregiver – doctor, nurse, family member and friend – is a minister of healing. Whether you are a caregiver by profession and/or a caregiver by pledge, you are a minster of healing. Whether you minister to the body, to the mind, to the spirit or to all three, you are a healer. To be whole and fully alive, the healthy self needs ministry in all three languages. 0- body mind and spirit.

Illness, suffering, pain, fatigue, exhaustion, fear, loss of hope, humiliation, offended pride, loneliness, lost faith in God or a good friend and a host of other shared physical and spiritual afflictions draw patients and their caregivers together in the mysterious ways of grace and God. Part of the mystery is that caregivers need tending also and often it is the ones they care for who tend to their spirits and bless them in their own distress. The sick are themselves ministers of healing, too. That is why these prayers and reflections are written to be shared by the sick ones and their caregivers. Patient and caregiver are partners in healing.

Whether patient or caregiver, we are healers. Our job, our work, is to heal. More than job or work, healing is our call. These prayers and thoughts acknowledge that the God who gives life to each one of us has called us to partner with Him in the care and healing of ourselves and of each other.

Over the years I have been many times impressed and blessed by my patients. I have found myself encouraged and healed by the ones to whom I have ministered. Both the caregiver and the patient are serving in ministry to each other as healing agents. The patient is quite often minister to the caregiver. *"Mercy is a double blessing. It blesses the one who gives it and the one who receives it."* (Shakespeare, The Merchant of Venice Act 4 Scene 1) Strength is needed by both for their service – hence the importance of these prayers. Peter's first letter reminds us that God supplies our need – *"Whoever serves, let it be with the strength that God supplies."* (1Peter 4:11)

Let me tell you a story. One day a nurse called me in the Chaplain's office and asked that I come visit a patient who had just been given a diagnosis of terminal cancer. I knocked on her door expecting to find someone distraught and in tears. Instead I met a serene, white-haired lady sitting up in bed with a prayer shawl wrapped around her shoulders and a smile on her face. A hospital volunteer had visited her earlier in the day and brought her the prayer shawl which was obviously giving her so much comfort right now. I said to her that I had heard of her diagnosis and had come to see if there was any comfort that I could offer her. She said to me: *"As long as I know that God is on His throne, I am alright!"* I was overwhelmed and blessed with awe at her faith. My own spirit was healed by this woman.

Prayer is first a conversation. Prayer is speaking (often in the language of poetry) and prayer is listening (usually in the language of the soul). Prayer is about connection and relationship.

The way I think about the language of prayer has everything to do with why I have written this book for you, my sisters and brothers. Our modern Western idea of prayer situates God far away in high heaven. Praying, then, seems a bit as if we have to take a megaphone and shout our needs up to Him - way up there – far distant – and then wait upon Him: first to see if He will even hear our prayer and then second to see if or how He will answer our prayer. That's it: we pray and then we wait. There is no conversation - God seems distant and somewhat indifferent in this model of prayer. He is fickle and only as caring as we project him to be. I have come to believe that prayer is something very different from this.

My idea of prayer is greatly influenced by the ancient Hebrew model of prayer: In this model God is near – not far. God is intimately interested and involved in what is happening in our life. Prayer is a search for His involved presence, for His companionship, for His Way. God is always assumed to be good and always acting for our good. God is never indifferent – always passionate for our good and never for our harm. God's will for us has nothing to do with whatever our present feelings may project upon him. He is measureless mercy and lasting love. No matter what the almighty God does, He cannot stop loving us!

Sickness throws trials and temptations that are both blatant and subtle into our prayer life. The experience of isolation and abandonment that often happens in sickness can block both prayer and hope. *"In the wilderness prepare the way of the LORD! Make straight in the wasteland a highway for our God!"* (Isaiah 40:3) The fruit of prayer is to make straight our paths – make level our ways. The path of right prayer stays in close relationship with God and searches for how He is present to us and involved in our present life situation! Prayer is a conversation that requires at least as much listening as it does speaking.

Prayer is done in a relationship marked by reverence and humility. The spiritual and emotional companionship of the patient and the caregiver is a powerful antidote to the personal isolation that can paralyze both in their healing efforts. Prayer is crucial to each in their companioning for healing. Illness can be the occasion of great isolation – a catalyst of pain and self-centering. It can also be the occasion of great intimacy – a catalyst of healing and of the experience of community: Healing always hinges on love. If isolation happens, love is blocked and our illness will complicate, deepen and prolong. If companioning happens, illness is ameliorated if not eliminated.

Illness and the care of the sick assault our privacy and sense of dignity. It seems our pride is undermined and challenged in our relationship with God and one another. Fences are broken down and are erected. Prayer is a positive way to reinforce and to rebuild our humility before God and in service to one another. Prayer is an action of relationship; it is a healing action in the face of illness and indignities that would harm our relationships and thus our wholeness and health.

Healing is not solitary. Healing happens best in companionship. Sometimes we are each other's "walkers" – in the sense of those actual metal contraptions that are designed to support us as we learn to stand and walk and keep our balance. We are also each other's "walkers" in the metaphor of the therapist who stands beside us and holds the gait belt in the middle of our back to prevent us from losing our balance and falling as we walk along. The point of being a walker for each other is to help each other carry our faith and carry our hope as we attempt to regain our spiritual and physical balance and wholeness when we are sick.

At times the caregiver carries a double or triple load of faith and hope – their own and their patient's and even that of the patient's families. We are healers. And with that comes many burdens on our own spirits. We cannot help but be touched to our soul by the plight of the sick, the injured, the grieving, the oppressed and the abused. It is our hope and our faith and our caring for each other that empower us and grace us to be good healers.

No matter what our job is in healthcare we are called here as healers. We listen to broken hearts with stethoscopes and with our ears. We look inside bodies with all sorts of technology; we look into souls with our eyes. We heal with medicine and love, compassion and prayer.

Our relationship to God has begun in His love and generosity. Our God is eternal and unchanging. We hope in His mercy. Pain and trouble can veil our ability to see and know God's presence and can deaden both our spirits and bodies. So let us be healers for each other today and make God's mercy and presence be seen and felt.

Individual health relies on the peace and good order of every one of the biological and chemical relationships within our bodies: individual health also relies on the peace and good order of all our relationships with self, with family, with the community and with our Creator, the Sustainer of our life. The states of our biological and our spirit health are parallel. Thus the compassion and reverence of our family, community and caregivers are catalysts to healing. The care giver and the sick person are in a relationship of covenanted hope, mutual faith and implicit trust in each other. Their relationship is an expression of community, a refutation of isolation. As Chief Seattle wrote, *"Humans did not weave the web of life – we each are merely a strand in it. Whatever we do to the web, we do to ourselves and to each other."*

CPSIA information can be obtained
at www.ICGtesting.com
Printed in the USA
BVOW09s2003061117
499662BV00028B/1391/P